Books
Business
Making Money Writing Books

John Monyjok Maluth

Copyright © 2024 John Monyjok Maluth

***

ISBN: 9798322010531

Discipleship Press

Web: www.discipleshippress.wordpress.com
Email: maluthabiel@gmail.com

~~***~~

+254 797 624 994

+211 927 145 394

P.O. Box 28448-00100, Nairobi Kenya

All rights reserved. No part of this book may be reproduced, stored in a retrieval system, or transmitted in any or by any means – electronic, mechanical, photocopying, recording, or otherwise-without prior permission in writing from the copyright holder.

DISCLAIMER:

This is a work of fiction. While inspired by real-world events, places, or concepts, the story and characters are entirely fictional. Any resemblance to actual persons, living or dead, or actual events is unintentional.

CONTENTS

CHAPTER 1: MY SWITCH FROM "WRITER" TO "PUBLISHER" 1

CHAPTER 2: THE BOOK BUSINESS MAP I FOLLOW EVERY TIME 10

CHAPTER 3: CHOOSING WHAT TO WRITE SO IT CAN ACTUALLY SELL 22

CHAPTER 4: BUILDING READERS BEFORE I PUSH BOOKS 36

CHAPTER 5: WRITING WITH BUSINESS DISCIPLINE, NOT MOOD 49

CHAPTER 6: STORY CRAFT THAT SELLS WITHOUT BEGGING 62

CHAPTER 7: PACKAGING THE BOOK LIKE A PRODUCT PEOPLE CAN TRUST 73

CHAPTER 8: THE MONEY MATH OF PUBLISHING 88

CHAPTER 9: PUBLISHING ROUTES AND THE TRADEOFFS I REFUSE TO IGNORE 104

CHAPTER 10: SELF-PUBLISHING STEP BY STEP, WITHOUT CONFUSION 119

CHAPTER 11: OFFLINE DISTRIBUTION THAT WORKS IN THE REAL WORLD 131

CHAPTER 12: ONLINE DISTRIBUTION AND DISCOVERABILITY 146

CHAPTER 13: MARKETING THAT DOES NOT DRAIN MY LIFE 162

CHAPTER 14: LAUNCH WEEK, THEN THE REAL WORK AFTER LAUNCH WEEK 177

CHAPTER 15: TURNING ONE BOOK INTO A CATALOG THAT EARNS YEAR AFTER YEAR **185**

CHAPTER 16: HANDLING DOUBT, CRITICISM, AND ENVY WITHOUT LOSING FOCUS **195**

CHAPTER 17: TRAINING OTHERS AND MULTIPLYING THE MARKET **205**

CHAPTER 18: THE LONG GAME, BUILDING A REAL PUBLISHING BUSINESS **217**

   APPENDICES: COPY-READY BUSINESS TOOLS 227
   FINAL NOTE TO THE READER 246

DISCLAIMER AND TEACHING NOTE

This book is a teaching story. The people you meet in these pages are examples built to carry real lessons about writing, publishing, and selling books as a serious business. The events and characters are fictional, even when they echo familiar places or struggles.

I write as Panyim, your guide. When you see Nyakor, Mama Ajok, Mr. Aldridge, Lila, and others, read them as "case studies in motion." They stand for the questions you will face, the doubts you will hear, and the decisions you must make when you choose to earn from books offline, online, or both.

Nothing here is legal, tax, or investment advice. I share methods, principles, and field-tested habits. You still must do your own checks for your country, your printing options, and your selling rules. What matters most is this: you can start small, stay honest, and grow step by step until your books become a stable income stream.

DEDICATION

I dedicate this book to the writer who has been told that stories cannot feed a household. To the teacher who wants to turn a skill into a living. To the young reader who has never owned a book, but is ready to carry one home like a treasure. And to every community that is hungry for words, knowledge, and hope.

HOW TO USE THIS BOOK

Read it twice, in two different ways.

On the first pass, read it like a story. Let the scenes move you. Let the struggles feel real. That first reading is for belief, and belief matters, because business is hard when your spirit is already defeated.

On the second pass, read it like a work manual. Keep a notebook beside you. After every major scene, stop and write what you would do if you were the one standing there. Then turn that answer into one small action you can finish within a day.

Choose your track early.

If you want an offline-first business, pay extra attention to how I build readers in the community, how I move books through schools, churches, events, and organizations, and how I handle bulk sales, receipts, and trust.

If you want an online-first business, pay extra attention to how I prepare a clean book product, how I make it discoverable, how I write descriptions that sell without noise, and how I keep marketing steady without burning out.

If you want the hybrid path, treat offline as your proof and online as your scale. Offline gives you cash flow and fast feedback. Online gives you reach and long-term sales while you sleep.

Use one simple operating rhythm as you read.

I write something. I improve something. I publish or distribute something. I talk to buyers or partners. I track what happened. Then I repeat.

That rhythm is how books stop being a dream and start becoming a business.

AUTHOR'S NOTE

I am not asking you to become famous. I am asking you to become consistent. A book business grows the way a library grows, one strong book at a time, one reader at a time, one honest sale at a time.

If you want, tell me to continue, and I will rewrite the next front-matter piece that should appear right after this: the "How this book is organized" page, followed by the table of contents page in a cleaner, more professional form.

CHAPTER 1: MY SWITCH FROM "WRITER" TO "PUBLISHER"

I did not become a publisher in a classroom. I became a publisher in the most ordinary place, inside that quiet moment after writing, when the last page is done and the heart is satisfied, yet the pocket is still empty. I had finished a manuscript and I was proud of it. The words were strong, the message was clean, and the story carried weight. I expected the world to respond as if my effort alone deserved a reward. That was my first mistake. Effort is not a sales plan. Effort is not distribution. Effort is not a business.

That day, I printed a few copies using what little I had. I carried them with a sense of dignity, as if holding paper was the same as holding a future. I showed the book to friends. They smiled. They praised my talent. They told me, "This is powerful," and "You are gifted," and "Keep going." I returned home feeling like I had won something. Then two weeks passed. No calls. No orders. No new buyers. No money returned to replace what I spent. I had applause, not customers.

The moment that changed me came when I asked myself a question I did not want to answer. If I keep writing like this, who will pay for the next book? If I keep printing like this, how will I recover the cost? If I keep giving away copies like gifts, how will I keep showing up in the world as a serious author? That question did not feel spiritual or poetic. It felt like hunger. It felt like reality walking into the room and sitting on my chair without permission.

I realized I had been living with a hidden belief. I believed that good writing sells itself. That belief is comforting, and it is also dangerous. It turns writers into beggars without them noticing. Because when your book does not sell itself, you start asking people to "support you." You start pleading for sympathy. You start blaming the market. And you start losing respect for your own work, not because the work is weak, but because you never built the bridge between the work and the buyer.

That is when I started seeing the difference between a manuscript and a product.

A manuscript is a completed message. It is the heart of what I want to say. It can be brilliant and still remain invisible. It can be true and still not reach the people who need it. It can be beautiful and still fail to feed the writer. A manuscript is not yet a business asset. It is raw value.

A product is that same value packaged, priced, positioned, and placed where a buyer can find it, trust it, and buy it without confusion. A product is not only words. It is words plus presentation. Words plus structure. Words plus access. Words plus a path from interest to purchase. A product respects the buyer's experience, not only the author's feelings.

That difference sounds simple, but it shook my mind. Because it meant my job was not finished when I typed "The End." My job was finished when a real reader could hold the book, understand what it offered, pay for it, and leave with the feeling that they received what they were promised. That is what business is. Business is delivery. Not talk. Not dreams. Delivery.

I began to examine my own habits with honest eyes. I saw that I had been writing like a man building a house without a door. The house might be strong, but people cannot enter. Then I would stand outside and shout, "Come in!" That is what many writers do. They create value, then they shout, then they get tired, then they give up. The real issue is not that people hate books. The issue is that people do not know what the book is, why it matters to them, and how to get it.

So I made a decision that became my switch from "writer" to "publisher." I decided that every book I create must earn its keep, not just inspire people.

Some people hear that and think I am reducing writing to money. I am not. I am protecting writing with money. If writing cannot sustain the writer, the writer becomes a part-time ghost, always disappearing into survival jobs, always postponing the next book, always tired, always delayed. I did not want that life. I wanted a life where my books could carry their own weight, and then carry me as well.

At that point, I started treating each book like a complete offer. I started asking business questions before I started writing.

Who is this for?
What problem does it solve or what desire does it fulfill?
Why should the buyer trust it?
Where will the buyer find it?
How will the buyer buy it?
How will the buyer receive it?

Those questions did not kill my creativity. They disciplined it. They gave my creativity direction. Instead of writing into the air, I began writing toward a real person.

This is where the characters in this book come in. When I introduce someone like Nyakor or Mama Ajok or Mr. Aldridge, I am not asking you to worship the character. I am using them as teaching examples. They represent the real buyers and real situations you will meet. They are mirrors. They are case studies in motion. They help you see how a business decision feels in a human moment.

For example, imagine a young teacher, Nyakor, who cares deeply about students but is tired of watching them fail due to poor study habits. She wants a book that can guide students with practical steps, not speeches. If I write a book for her, my job is not to impress her with vocabulary. My job is to give her a clear tool she can use in class. If I succeed, she buys. If she buys and sees results, she recommends it to other teachers. That is how a product moves. Not through noise, but through usefulness.

Now imagine another buyer, Mama Ajok, who is not thinking about "reading culture." She is thinking about survival and family. She will not buy a book because it is "important." She will buy a book because it solves a problem she feels every day. If I do not understand her, I will keep blaming the market. If I do understand her, I will package and position my message in a way that matches her life.

This is why a publisher must have empathy, not only talent. Empathy is business intelligence. It tells you what the buyer will pay for and what the buyer will ignore.

Once I accepted that, I wrote my personal rule, and it became the backbone of everything I publish.

Every book must have a clear buyer, a clear promise, and a clear path to market.

A clear buyer means I can describe the reader in one clean sentence. Not "everyone." Not "people who love books." A real buyer has a face. A life. A problem. A desire. A schedule. A budget. A reason. If I cannot name that person, I am writing blind.

When I say "clear buyer," I do not mean I must know the buyer's name. I mean I must know the buyer's type. Who are they? What stage of life are they in? What do they struggle with? What do they want? What language do they use to describe their problem? What are they willing to pay for? Where do they hang out, offline or online?

This one shift stopped me from wasting months on books that were not ready to be sold. It also stopped me from writing titles that sounded clever but were useless in a marketplace. Because a buyer does not wake up in the morning searching for cleverness. A buyer wakes up searching for help, meaning, and relief.

A clear promise means the book gives a result the reader can understand before buying. The promise is not a lie. It is not exaggeration. It is the real value the book delivers. If the book is a business guide, the promise might be a step by step method to build income with books. If the book is a memoir, the promise might be a story of survival that offers courage and direction. If the book is a personal growth book, the promise might be a habit system that builds discipline.

A promise is the answer to a silent question in the buyer's mind: what do I get if I read this?

If your promise is vague, your marketing will be vague. If your marketing is vague, people will delay. If people delay, they forget. Then your book sits. Many authors think the market is cruel, when the real issue is that the offer is unclear.

This is why I treat the promise statement as a business tool. It becomes the backbone of the cover and description. It shapes the title and subtitle. It shapes the chapter flow. It keeps me from writing random chapters that do not serve the reader.

A clear path to market means I decide how the book will travel from my hands to the buyer's hands.

This is the part most writers avoid, and this is why most writers stay broke. They write, they print, they post a photo, they wait. Waiting is not a path. Waiting is surrender.

A path to market can be offline, online, or both. It can be built through schools, churches, offices, events, bookstores, and bulk partners. It can be built through online stores, direct links, email lists, and content that attracts readers. But it must be a real path, not a wish.

When I say "path," I mean practical answers.

Where will the book be available?
What format will it be in, print, ebook, or both?
What payment methods will I accept?
How will delivery happen?

What is my follow up plan after a sale?
How will I restock if I run out?
How will I track money and stock so I do not lose control?

This rule changed how I viewed "publishing." Publishing stopped being a badge and became a system.

And once I treated publishing as a system, I became calmer. I stopped feeling like I needed the whole world to approve. I only needed to serve the right buyers and keep building channels that work.

This is also where I learned a second truth that many writers do not want to hear. Your book is not competing with other books only. Your book is competing with everything else in your buyer's life. The buyer has bills. The buyer has family issues. The buyer has phone distractions. The buyer has fatigue. The buyer has fear. If your product does not look clear and valuable, it will lose to scrolling.

That is why the manuscript must become a product. A product makes the buyer's decision easy.

So how did my behavior change after the switch?

I stopped writing titles first. I started writing promises first.
I stopped printing first. I started planning channels first.
I stopped giving away copies like a man asking for love. I started using copies with intention, as part of a sales plan.
I stopped announcing a book like news. I started offering a book like a solution.

I stopped measuring success by praise. I started measuring success by sales, repeat buyers, and referrals.

That last one is important. Praise is sweet, but it is unstable. Sales are not only money. Sales are proof that the book mattered enough for someone to exchange value for it. When a person buys, they are voting with money. When they buy again, they are voting with trust. When they recommend, they are voting with reputation.

This is why I say a book must earn its keep. A book that earns its keep is a book that is doing its job in the world.

Now let me speak to the writer who fears that business thinking will poison the purity of writing.

Business thinking does not poison writing. Fear poisons writing. Confusion poisons writing. Poverty poisons writing. When you are constantly worried about survival, you rush. When you rush, quality drops. When quality drops, trust drops. When trust drops, sales drop. Then you suffer again. That cycle is brutal.

A clean business approach breaks that cycle. It gives you time to write better. It gives you resources to edit properly. It gives you peace to publish consistently. And it gives you the ability to serve more readers without begging.

I am not teaching you to chase money like a thief. I am teaching you to build a life where your work is respected and paid for, so you can keep creating without shame.

At the end of this chapter, I want you to do a simple exercise. Do it honestly, not beautifully.

Write one sentence that begins with: This book is for…

Finish the sentence with a real buyer type, not a dream crowd.

Then write one sentence that begins with: This book helps you…

Finish it with the real result your buyer gets.

Then write one sentence that begins with: You can buy it by…

Finish it with the first path you will use, even if it is small.

Those three sentences are your first publishing declaration. They turn a manuscript into a product plan.

When you have those three, you have already crossed the line I crossed. You are no longer only writing to express yourself. You are writing to deliver value to a buyer, through a real channel, with a clear promise.

That is the switch.

That is how a writer becomes a publisher.

And once you become a publisher, you stop waiting for permission. You start building a catalog that can carry your mission and your income forward, one honest book at a time.

CHAPTER 2: THE BOOK BUSINESS MAP I FOLLOW EVERY TIME

After I made the switch from writer to publisher, I faced a new danger. I could easily become busy without becoming effective. I could write more, print more, post more, talk more, and still remain stuck in the same financial place. That is what happens when a person has energy but no system. Energy can look impressive, but without direction it becomes exhaustion.

So I built a map.

Not a complicated map. Not a map that requires a big team. A map I could follow when life is noisy, when money is tight, when power is unreliable, when the internet is weak, and when people are skeptical. A map that could survive real conditions.

That map became the backbone of my book business, and it is the map I return to every time I feel lost.

Create. Package. Distribute. Sell. Repeat.

Five stages. One cycle. No confusion.

When I treat my work as a cycle, I stop thinking that success comes from one big moment. I stop dreaming of a single launch that changes everything. Instead, I build a machine that produces results through consistency.

Let me walk you through each stage the way I live it, not the way people talk about it.

CREATE

Create means I produce the actual value. This is the writing stage, but not only writing. It includes selecting the right idea, outlining it, drafting, and finishing the manuscript in a way that serves a clear buyer and a clear promise.

Creation is where many people get stuck because they think creativity is mysterious. They wait for inspiration, and they confuse waiting with preparation. I do not wait. I schedule. I write. I revise. I finish.

The business reason creation matters is simple. If you cannot finish books, you cannot build assets. Without assets, you cannot build income. You may talk about books all day, but talk does not pay printing costs.

So in creation I focus on three things.

First, the buyer. I keep the reader in mind. I do not write for applause. I write for outcomes.

Second, the promise. I do not allow the book to wander. Every chapter must serve the promise.

Third, completion. A finished manuscript is the only kind that can be packaged, distributed, and sold.

This is where I remind myself that a half written book is not a dream. It is a debt. It sits in the mind like unpaid rent. Finishing clears space, and clear space is where the next book is born.

PACKAGE

Packaging is where the manuscript becomes a product. This is the stage most writers disrespect, and then they complain when sales are weak.

Packaging includes editing, proofreading, formatting, cover design, title and subtitle clarity, and the description that explains the offer.

Packaging is trust in visible form. Buyers do not only buy words. They buy confidence. They buy professionalism. They buy the feeling that the author respects them enough to deliver something clean.

I learned to treat packaging as a business investment, not as decoration.

If I skip editing, I save money today and pay with bad reviews tomorrow.
If I skip good design, I save time today and pay with lost clicks tomorrow.
If I rush formatting, I publish quickly and pay with reader frustration tomorrow.

So I package patiently, because packaging protects the long term.

When people open a book and feel calm, they keep reading.
When they keep reading, they finish.
When they finish, they recommend.
When they recommend, the book sells with less effort.

That is how packaging becomes marketing without noise.

DISTRIBUTE

Distribution is where most authors fail silently.

They think publishing is distribution.
They think uploading is distribution.
They think printing is distribution.

It is not.

Distribution means placement. It means availability where the buyer actually buys.

Offline distribution means shops, schools, churches, offices, events, libraries, community centers, and bulk partners.

Online distribution means marketplaces, search discoverability, category placement, and direct links that lead to a clean listing or a direct sales page.

Distribution is also logistics. Stock. Delivery. Payment method. Terms. Records.

If you do not build distribution, your book remains a private possession. It may be a beautiful possession, but it is still private.

This stage is where I think like a shop owner. Where will the product sit? How will a buyer find it? How will a buyer take it home? How will I get paid and track it?

SELL

Selling is the stage writers fear because they misunderstand it.

They think selling is begging.
They think selling is manipulation.
They think selling makes them look desperate.

That happens only when you are selling without clarity and without value.

Selling, when done right, is guiding the right person to the right book.

Selling means conversations, offers, and follow up. It means invitations, not pressure. It means being clear about price, clear about value, clear about who the book is for, and clear about how to buy.

Selling is also the stage where the business breathes. No sales means no cash flow. No cash flow means no reprints, no editing budgets, no growth.

So I do not romanticize selling. I respect selling as a service activity. If the book helps someone, I have a responsibility to make the offer visible.

REPEAT

Repeat is the secret that separates hobby authors from business authors.

Many people can write one book.
Many people can launch one book.
Many people can make noise for one week.

But repeating is what builds wealth, skill, and stability.

Repeating means I do not stop after one title.
Repeating means I do not wait for perfect conditions to start the next book.
Repeating means I improve the system each cycle.

This is how a catalog is born.

One book is a door.
A catalog is a neighborhood.
A neighborhood attracts traffic.

When you repeat, you stop feeling that every book must be a miracle. You allow books to work together. One title sells another. One topic leads to a deeper topic. One buyer becomes a repeat buyer. The pressure spreads, and your business becomes stronger.

Now, I want to show you how this cycle works in three routes, because many people get confused and think they must do everything at once.

OFFLINE ROUTE

In the offline route, the cycle looks like this.

Create: I write with a clear local buyer in mind. I think about the setting, the language, the daily realities, the problems people discuss face to face.

Package: I prepare a printed book with clean design and durable binding, because physical handling matters.

Distribute: I place copies in shops, schools, churches, offices, and events. I negotiate consignment or wholesale terms. I build partner relationships.

Sell: I sell through in person sessions, talks, workshops, community gatherings, and direct conversations. I use receipts and tracking.

Repeat: I restock based on sales speed. I schedule the next event. I write the next book that the local market proves it needs.

Offline is powerful because trust is built quickly. People see you, hear you, and touch the product. In markets where internet is weak, offline can be the strongest engine of cash flow.

But offline also requires discipline. If you do not track stock and money, you will lose control. If you do not build relationships, you will keep carrying books like a traveler carrying luggage with no destination.

ONLINE ROUTE

In the online route, the cycle looks like this.

Create: I write with a buyer who searches online. I think about the phrases they type, the results they want, the "beginner" problems, and the steps they crave.

Package: I prepare ebook and print files, clean cover readability for thumbnail, strong description, and professional formatting.

Distribute: I publish on online marketplaces and build direct links. I set categories and keywords with buyer intent.

Sell: I sell through content, email, social posts, reviews, and steady traffic building. I focus on conversion, not only visibility.

Repeat: I update metadata when needed, improve the book when feedback reveals issues, then publish the next book to expand the catalog and improve discoverability.

Online is powerful because it scales. It reaches beyond geography. It works while you sleep. It can create steady income over time, especially when you have a catalog.

But online also punishes carelessness. Bad packaging leads to bad reviews. Bad metadata leads to invisibility. Hope leads to silence.

HYBRID ROUTE

The hybrid route is the route I love for stability, because it gives me proof and reach.

Create: I write a book that serves both local and global readers, with clear examples and clear language.

Package: I design it so it looks professional in print and online.

Distribute: I place it offline in key channels and also publish it online for wider reach.

Sell: I use offline events to build trust and create stories and photos and testimonials. I use online content to scale that trust and reach new buyers.

Repeat: I let offline cash flow fund better packaging and more production, while online discoverability keeps working quietly in the background.

Hybrid is not "more work for nothing." Hybrid is risk management. If one channel slows down, the other can hold you. If the market changes, you are not trapped.

Now that you understand the cycle and the routes, let me give you the minimum business setup a serious author needs.

This is the part people often overcomplicate. They think they need a company office, a big staff, expensive software, or perfect branding before they begin. That is delay disguised as professionalism.

A serious author needs only a few essentials to start.

A clear identity
You must know what you write and who you serve. This does not mean you cannot grow later. It means you can explain yourself now. When people ask, "What do you write?" you must answer in one sentence that makes sense.

A basic product kit
You need a clean manuscript, a professional cover, proper formatting, and a description that communicates the

promise. If your product kit is weak, everything else becomes harder.

A channel plan
You need one primary channel to start. One. Not ten. One strong channel is better than many weak channels. For offline, that might be schools and events. For online, that might be one marketplace plus email. Pick one and build it until it works.

A simple tracking system
This is non negotiable. If you want books as a business, you must track.

For offline, track:
Stock in hand.
Stock placed with partners.
Copies sold.
Cash received.
Money owed.
Reprint point.

For online, track:
Sales by title.
What content or channel drives sales.
Which books convert best.
Basic monthly trends.

You can do this with a notebook, a spreadsheet, or a simple sheet. The tool is not the point. The habit is the point.

A routine that protects production and promotion
A book business dies when you only write or only market. You need both.

I keep it simple.
I write on a schedule.
I promote on a schedule.
I review weekly.

Even if the schedule is small, it must exist.

Integrity as an operational policy
People treat integrity like a moral speech. I treat it like a business asset.

If you deliver what you promise, buyers return.
If you keep records, partners trust you.
If you price fairly, you build long term sales.
If you respect readers, your reputation grows.

A business without integrity becomes a hustle, and a hustle collapses when the first storm comes.

Now let me make this chapter practical with a scene, because this is how I teach.

Imagine a young author who finishes a manuscript and prints fifty copies without planning anything else. He carries them around like a trophy. He goes to a friend's office. People praise him. Two people buy. He returns home discouraged. He begins to think books do not sell.

Now imagine the same author with the map.

He creates with a clear buyer.
He packages professionally.
He distributes through one channel first, maybe schools.
He sells through a workshop offer.

He tracks sales and stock.
He repeats.

In the first story, the author is a traveler with luggage.
In the second story, the author is a merchant with a route.

That is the difference a map makes.

Before you move to Chapter 3 in your own journey, I want you to write your map on one page.

Write the five stages.

Under each stage, write one action you will take in the next seven days.

Create: what will I write or finish?
Package: what will I improve or prepare?
Distribute: where will I place the book or listing?
Sell: who will I contact or what offer will I present?
Repeat: what is my next cycle goal and how will I track it?

If you can do this weekly, you will stop feeling lost.
You will stop guessing.
And you will start building a book business that survives real life, not only good days.

That is the Book Business Map I follow every time.

CHAPTER 3: CHOOSING WHAT TO WRITE SO IT CAN ACTUALLY SELL

When I was younger in this work, I believed the hardest part was writing the book. I believed once the pages were finished, the market would respond like a hungry man responding to food. That belief sounded noble, but it was blind. The truth is that many books fail before the first chapter is drafted. They fail at selection. They fail because the author chose a topic that nobody is searching for, nobody is asking for, and nobody is willing to pay for. Or the author chose a topic that is needed, but the author has no real authority to teach it, so the result is weak, confusing, and forgettable.

This chapter is where I teach you how I choose what to write so it can actually sell, both offline and online, without turning you into a person who chases every trend. I am not teaching you to write like a robot. I am teaching you to write like a publisher who respects readers, respects time, and respects the money math we discussed earlier.

I use two anchors every time I choose a book.

Reader demand.
Personal authority.

If you hold these two anchors properly, you stop writing into the air. You start writing toward a real buyer.

Reader demand means there is a real hunger for the thing you plan to offer. Personal authority means you can deliver that offer with truth, skill, and responsibility. When both are present, selling becomes easier because you are not forcing a product into a cold market. You are meeting a need with a credible solution.

Let me start with reader demand, because demand is often misunderstood.

Many writers think demand is only what is popular on the internet. They see viral topics and they panic. They start thinking, "If I do not write about this, I will miss the moment." That is not demand. That is noise. Noise comes fast and dies fast. Demand is different. Demand is what keeps returning, week after week, month after month, because it is tied to human problems that do not disappear.

Demand is what makes a person say, "I need help."
Demand is what makes a person ask, "Do you have a book on this?"
Demand is what makes a person search, "How do I do this?"
Demand is what makes a teacher say, "My students keep failing at this."
Demand is what makes a parent say, "My child needs this."
Demand is what makes a young worker say, "I am stuck and I need a path."

I listen for those signals like a shopkeeper listens for footsteps.

Offline demand is heard in speech.
Online demand is seen in search and behavior.

Offline, I listen to the questions people ask in gatherings, offices, schools, churches, and ordinary conversations. I listen to the same complaints repeating from different mouths. When the same pain keeps showing up, I know there is a book hiding there.

Online, I watch the phrases people use when they are looking for solutions. I watch what kinds of posts get saved, shared, or commented on with real questions. I watch what people pay for already, because money spent is one of the strongest proofs of demand.

Demand also shows up in what people borrow. In many places, readers may not buy quickly, but they borrow. If a certain kind of book keeps being borrowed, that is a strong signal. Borrowing is not "free interest." Borrowing is a sign that the subject matters enough for people to invest time. When people invest time, money can follow if the product is positioned correctly.

Now let me show you a simple way I test demand before I commit months of my life to writing.

I ask myself: can I name ten real people who have this problem right now?

Not ten people who might like it someday. Ten people who are already talking about it. Ten people who are already asking for help. Ten people whose lives would improve if this book existed.

If I cannot name ten, I slow down. I either refine the topic, or I accept that it is a passion book that may not sell fast. Passion books can still be worth writing, but I must be honest about what they are. Business books must be built with demand in mind.

Then I ask: do people already pay for solutions related to this problem?

They might pay for classes, subscriptions, coaching, data, travel, tools, or services. If money is already being spent in that direction, demand exists. If nobody spends money and nobody searches and nobody asks, I must ask a hard question. Am I building a product, or am I building a monument to my own feelings?

This is where many writers get offended. They want the market to love what they love. They want the world to applaud their inner life. I understand that desire, because I have felt it. But I also learned something that saved me. The market does not reject you as a human. The market only rejects unclear offers.

When you accept that, you become calmer. You stop taking silence personally. You start treating silence as feedback.

Now let me speak about personal authority, because demand alone is not enough.

If you chase demand without authority, you become a shallow seller. You can write something that looks right on the surface, but it will not carry depth, it will not carry lived truth, and it will not carry a voice that readers can trust. That kind of book may get a few sales, but it will not build a name. It will not build referrals. It will not build a catalog that lasts.

Authority is not perfection. Authority is the right to guide.

I measure my authority in three ways.

Have I lived this?
Have I studied this deeply enough to teach it responsibly?
Have I tested this in real life with results, either for myself or for others?

If at least one of these is strong, and the other two are not weak, I can write. If all three are weak, I pause. I either do the work to build authority, or I choose another topic.

Let me give you an example using a character, because characters make these choices visible.

Nyakor is a young educator. She wants to write a book on study skills. Demand is obvious. Students struggle. Parents complain. Teachers worry. But Nyakor must still ask about authority. Has she actually helped students improve? Has she tested methods that work in her setting? Can she teach beyond motivational talk?

If Nyakor has real experience guiding students, she has authority. If she only likes the idea of being seen as an education writer, she does not have authority yet. In that case, her first step is to coach a group of students, record what works, collect stories of improvement, then write from tested truth. That is how authority is built.

Now consider Mr. Aldridge, an office manager who wants to write about leadership. Demand exists. Organizations want better leaders. But authority matters. If he has never led a team, never managed conflict, and never built a working system, his book will be thin. He may impress people with quotes, but he will not help them. Readers are tired of quotes that do not change anything.

Authority is what allows you to write for outcomes rather than for applause.

Now we come to the part that many writers dislike, because it challenges ego.

How do I avoid writing for applause and instead write for outcomes?

The first thing I do is I stop using praise as my compass.

Praise is easy to get when you write sentences that sound deep. You can write a paragraph that makes people say, "Wow." But a "wow" does not mean the reader knows what to do next. It does not mean the reader can change anything. It only means you created a feeling.

Feelings matter, but business needs results.

So I ask a different question.

What will the reader be able to do, think, or handle better after reading this book?

That question forces me to write with intent. It forces me to design the book like a tool, even if it is told through story.

When I write for outcomes, my chapters become clearer. My examples become sharper. My teaching becomes more practical. My reader feels guided rather than impressed.

Writing for applause often produces vague writing.
Writing for outcomes produces clear writing.

Applause writing avoids risk. It tries to please everyone. Outcome writing takes a stand. It chooses a buyer and serves them well.

Applause writing hides behind complex language. Outcome writing explains with plain strength.

Applause writing says, "Look at my mind."
Outcome writing says, "Here is your next step."

This is why outcome writing sells better. It respects the buyer's needs.

Now, there is another reason I avoid applause writing. Applause is unstable.

You can be praised today and ignored tomorrow.
You can be celebrated in one room and criticized in another.
You can be called "gifted" and still be broke.

If I build my publishing life on applause, I will be emotionally controlled by strangers. That is not freedom. That is slavery in a polite suit.

So I built a new way of measuring success.

Did the book reach the right buyer?
Did the book deliver its promise?
Did buyers recommend it to others?
Did it create repeat buyers?

Those measures are not emotional. They are practical. They keep me focused.

Now let me teach you the key tool that ties demand and authority into one clean offer.

The promise statement.

The promise statement is the backbone of your cover and description. It is the sentence that allows a stranger to understand what they are buying. It is the bridge between your book and the buyer's decision.

When the promise statement is clear, everything becomes easier.
The title becomes easier.
The subtitle becomes easier.
The cover design becomes easier.
The description becomes easier.
The marketing message becomes easier.
The chapter plan becomes easier.

When the promise statement is unclear, you struggle everywhere. You keep rewriting titles. You keep changing covers. You keep posting random messages. You keep feeling like your book is "good" but nobody understands it. That confusion often comes from a missing promise.

So I write a promise statement early, and I treat it like a contract.

It is not a marketing trick. It is a truth statement about what the book will deliver.

Here are the forms I use. I will show you several so you can choose what fits your style.

A direct promise statement:

This book helps (who) to (result) by (method) so they can (benefit).

A simple buyer promise:

For (who) who want to (result) without (pain or obstacle).

A story-led promise:

This story is for (who) who want to (feel or understand) and learn (lesson) so they can (life change).

A practical guide promise:

A step-by-step guide to (result) for (who), built for (setting), without (common frustration).

Now let me put flesh on those bones with examples, because examples make it real.

If I am writing a book on building a book business offline, my promise might be:

This book helps new and working authors turn one manuscript into a selling product, using simple offline distribution, pricing, and repeatable routines, so they can earn steady income without begging.

If I am writing a study skills guide, my promise might be:

For students who want to study smarter, remember more, and pass exams without panic or last-minute cramming.

If I am writing a story-led personal discipline book, my promise might be:

This story is for anyone who keeps starting and stopping, and wants to learn how discipline is built through small daily minimums, so they can become consistent without waiting for motivation.

You can feel the difference. The promise is not "This is a great book." The promise is "Here is what you will get."

Now, I use demand and authority to sharpen the promise.

Demand tells me what result readers want most.
Authority tells me what result I can deliver honestly.

If demand says people want "make money from books," but my authority is only "I wrote one book and sold five copies," then my promise must be smaller and more honest, like "how to sell your first fifty copies locally," not "how to build a publishing empire." Truth sells better long term than exaggeration.

This is also where many authors trap themselves with promises that are too broad.

When your promise is too broad, your book becomes a general talk. General talk does not sell well to strangers. Strangers buy specific solutions.

So I narrow my promise until it feels like a clear target.

Instead of "How to build a business," I might write "How to build a book business that sells offline in schools and events."

Instead of "How to write better," I might write "How to finish your first draft with daily minimums and weekly checkpoints."

Instead of "How to market," I might write "How to promote one book each week without draining your life."

Narrow promises attract the right buyers. Broad promises attract nobody strongly.

Now, how does the promise become the backbone of the cover and description?

Let me teach you how I translate promise into packaging.

The cover is not a summary. The cover is a signal.

The cover must communicate three things fast.

What this is.
Who it is for.
What result it gives.

You do that through title and subtitle clarity and through visual cues that match genre.

If your promise is practical, your cover must look practical.
If your promise is story-led, your cover must look story-led.
If your promise is academic, your cover must look academic.

When the cover signal matches the promise, buyers feel safe. Safety increases clicks and buys.

Now the description.

A strong description is your promise expanded and proven.

I structure my description like a clear conversation.

I begin with the buyer's pain and desire.
I state the promise in simple language.
I explain what is inside, in a way that feels organized.
I show why the reader should trust me.
I close with what to do next.

If my promise is clear, the description almost writes itself. If my promise is unclear, the description becomes a confused essay about my personal journey. Personal journey has a place, but a buyer first wants to know what they get.

Now let me show you my method for picking a topic or story, step by step, without turning this chapter into a lecture full of theory.

I start with an idea bank.
I keep a running list of problems people ask me about, problems I have solved, and topics I have lived deeply. I do not judge the list. I collect.

Then I run each idea through the demand filter.
Who is asking for this?
How often does it appear?
Where does it appear, schools, offices, online messages, groups?
Do people pay for related solutions already?

Then I run it through the authority filter.
What have I lived here?
What have I tested here?
What can I teach without pretending?

Then I combine both and choose the strongest match. Sometimes the strongest match is not the topic I love most emotionally. It is the topic that can serve a real buyer now while still fitting my voice.

This is a mature decision. It is the decision that turns writing into a business.

Now, there is another trap I want you to avoid.

Some authors choose topics based on what makes them look intelligent. They want to sound like scholars even when their readers are ordinary people trying to survive daily life. They choose fancy subjects that have no clear buyer. Then they complain when sales are slow.

I am not against big ideas. I write big ideas too. But I package big ideas in a way that serves a buyer.

If the buyer is a busy young worker, I write with clarity and direct usefulness.
If the buyer is a student, I write with step-by-step guidance.
If the buyer is an advanced reader, I can go deeper, but I still must remain clear.

You must know who you are writing for. Otherwise you will write a book that looks like a speech delivered to an empty hall.

Let me close this chapter with a final truth.

A book that sells is not always the loudest book.
A book that sells is often the clearest book.
A book that sells is the book that matches a real need and is written by someone who can deliver the promise.

That is why I choose topics with demand and authority, not with pride and applause.

Now here is your exercise, and I want you to do it seriously.

Write three possible topics you want to write next.
For each one, write who the buyer is in one sentence.
Then write a one-sentence promise statement for each.
Then ask yourself which promise you can deliver with the strongest honesty and which buyer is most real in your life right now.

When you choose that book, you are no longer writing a guess.
You are building a product with a market.

That is how publishers choose what to write.

CHAPTER 4: BUILDING READERS BEFORE I PUSH BOOKS

There is a reason many good books die quietly. It is not always because the writing is weak. It is because the author tries to sell books in a place where buying books is not yet a habit. In such a place, you can stand on the road with a stack of copies and a brave smile, and still go home with the same stack. You can post the cover on your phone and collect likes and praise, and still remain stuck. You can even be called "a great writer" and still not pay your printing bill. That is the pain that forced me to learn a deeper truth. Before I push books, I build readers.

When I say "build readers," I do not mean I try to change the whole country. I mean I create small pockets of reading life where trust can grow, where buying becomes normal, and where word of mouth can travel faster than my own voice. If reading is weak or inconsistent, I do not fight the whole culture like a man wrestling the wind. I work like a farmer. I choose a small plot. I plant. I water. I protect. I harvest. Then I expand.

The biggest mistake I see is this. An author assumes that the market is already warm. They assume people wake up thinking about buying books. In many places, that is not true. People wake up thinking about food, rent, school fees, transport, medical bills, safety, and family pressure. Reading might be respected, but it is often not purchased. It is treated as a luxury or as something only students do when forced. If you do not accept that reality, you will take rejection personally, and bitterness will grow inside you like mold.

So I learned to build demand the same way a good teacher builds understanding. Step by step, in human settings, with repetition and trust.

Demand, in weak reading environments, is not created by shouting "Buy my book." Demand is created by three simple forces working together: exposure, usefulness, and community.

Exposure means people must meet the book again and again until it becomes familiar. Most buyers do not purchase on the first contact, especially when money is tight. They watch you. They test your seriousness. They want to know if you will still be here next month. That is why one launch event does not create a reading market. It only creates a moment.

Usefulness means the book must solve something real. If your book is only inspiring but not practical, some people will clap, but fewer will buy. People spend money more easily when the value is clear and immediate. Even when your book is a story, the reader must feel that the story leaves them with something they can carry into life.

Community means reading must feel social, not lonely. In many places, people will attend a gathering faster than they will sit alone with a book. They will join a group faster than they will commit to a private habit. That is not weakness. That is human nature. Community lowers the fear of "wasting money." Community also adds pride. People like to belong to something that makes them feel intelligent, respected, and connected.

Once I understood these three forces, I stopped selling like a street hawker and started building like a publisher.

Let me show you how I create demand where reading is weak.

I begin with what I call public teaching. I give away a small portion of value in public, not as charity, but as proof. I speak one lesson. I tell one story. I share one tool. I answer a few questions. Then I let the book appear as the deeper version of what they just received. I am not begging. I am guiding. I am saying, "If this helped you in fifteen minutes, the book will help you further."

This is how I convert attention into trust. People do not buy because you wrote a book. They buy because they believe the book will help them. That belief is built through experience, not through claims.

There was a time I visited a small community gathering and spoke about discipline. I did not mention my book at first. I asked a simple question: why do we keep starting and stopping? People laughed because they recognized themselves. Then I told a short story about my own struggle to finish projects when life was noisy. I shared one practical method: choose a daily minimum that you can keep even on bad days. I asked them to name their own daily minimum for one week. Only after that did I show the book. The room changed. The book was no longer a stranger. It was a tool connected to a real moment. Many who would not buy from a poster bought from that experience.

This is the foundation. I do not sell a book. I sell a result. The book is the container.

Now I will walk you through the places I use to build readers and turn interest into buying habits: small gatherings, schools, churches, offices, and clubs. Each place has its own psychology, and if you ignore that psychology, you will struggle.

Small gatherings are my first engine because they are intimate and fast. In a small gathering, people can see my face, hear my voice, ask questions, and measure my sincerity. Trust forms quickly when people can test you in real time. I do not need a microphone. I do not need a stage. I need a circle and a clear lesson.

I keep small gatherings simple. I choose one topic that matches my book promise. I teach for a short time. I invite discussion. I answer questions. Then I offer the book as an option, not as pressure. I also make buying easy. Clear price. Simple payment. A copy in their hands. If you make buying complicated, they postpone, and postponement is the silent killer of sales.

I also learned to respect the dignity of the buyer. When money is tight, some people want the book but feel shy. They do not want to be the one asking for a discount in public. So I quietly create options. I might offer a group discount if friends buy together. I might offer a bundle. I might allow a trusted person to collect money privately and bring one payment. The goal is not to squeeze people. The goal is to build the habit of buying books without shame.

Schools are my strongest long-term engine because schools already have structure. Teachers have goals. Students have pressure. Parents have hopes. If your book can serve a school goal, the school can become a steady channel.

But I do not walk into a school like a man selling perfume. I walk in like a professional bringing a tool. I ask what the students struggle with. I ask what the teachers want to improve. Then I position the book as support for outcomes: better writing, better study routines, better discipline, better leadership, or whatever your book offers.

Let me give you an example. Nyakor, a teacher, is not looking for poetry on a random day. She is looking for something that can help her students pass exams, write better, or behave better. If I bring a book and say, "Support me," she might smile and forget me. If I bring a short session and say, "Here are three study habits that can help your students improve," she listens. If I show her how the book can be used as a class tool, she starts thinking as a buyer, not as a supporter.

When schools become your channel, bulk sales become possible. A school might buy for a class set. A sponsor might fund copies for students. A club might buy as prizes. Even one school can create repeat orders if the book proves useful.

But schools require patience and respect. You must be reliable. You must deliver copies on time. You must keep your word. Nothing kills school trust faster than an author who promises and disappears.

Churches are powerful in weak reading environments because churches gather people consistently. Many people attend services even when they do not read books. That means churches can become a gateway to reading habits if you approach with respect.

I do not treat a church like a marketplace. I treat it like a community of values. I speak with leadership first. I ask permission. I offer service first. I might teach on a topic that matches the church's needs: family stability, integrity, discipline, leadership, forgiveness, purpose, or practical life skills. Then I make the book available after the service in a calm way.

The church setting also helps because people trust recommendations there. If a pastor or a leader says, "This book helped me," the book gains weight. But I never chase endorsements like a desperate man. I let value earn trust. People can smell manipulation in spiritual spaces. I refuse that.

Offices and organizations are overlooked, yet they hold strong buying power. In offices, people deal with practical problems: communication, leadership, ethics, productivity, conflict, and career growth. They also have teams, which makes bulk buying easier.

When I approach an office, I do not talk like a poet. I talk like a builder. I offer a lunch session or a short workshop. I connect the book to the office goal. If the office is struggling with performance, I speak about discipline and consistency. If the office is struggling with communication, I speak about clarity and responsibility. Then I offer the book as a team tool.

The key with offices is professionalism. Receipts. Clear terms. Delivery schedule. Follow-up. Once an office trusts you, they become a referral source to other offices. One manager tells another manager. That is how word of mouth spreads in professional circles.

Clubs are where reading becomes identity. A club could be a youth group, a women's group, a writers' group, an entrepreneurship circle, or even a simple monthly gathering of friends. Clubs are powerful because they create repetition without forcing it. When the group meets regularly, the book is not a one-time event. It becomes part of a rhythm.

In a club setting, I often use a "chapter and discussion" approach. We take one chapter, discuss the lesson, share experiences, then set one action step for the week. This approach does two things. It makes reading social and it makes the book feel alive. People become invested, and invested readers become promoters.

Now, you might ask, how do I turn interest into buying habits?

Interest is easy to get. Habits are harder. Habits require repeated behavior with low friction. So I reduce friction.

I make the book easy to understand. The buyer must know what they get.
I make the price and payment easy. Confusion kills action.
I make the purchase feel respectable. Buying should feel like joining something meaningful, not like being squeezed.
I make follow-up normal. People buy again when they feel seen.

I also learned to build what I call the "small ladder."

Most people will not jump from zero to "I buy books every month." But they can climb a ladder.

The first step might be attending a talk.
The next step might be reading a short sample.
The next step might be buying one book.
The next step might be bringing a friend.
The next step might be joining a club.
The next step might be buying a second book.

When you build a ladder, you stop being frustrated with slow buyers. You guide them forward.

One of my favorite methods is the sample chapter method. I do not give away the whole book. I give away a clean taste. One chapter that carries the heart of the promise. If the chapter is strong, it creates hunger. If the chapter is weak, it exposes a bigger problem, which is good because it forces me to improve.

I also use what I call visible ownership. When a person buys a book, I treat it as an achievement. I sign the copy. I write their name. If they want, we take a photo. Not for vanity, but for pride. Pride creates identity. Identity creates habit. When someone feels proud of owning a book, they are more likely to read it, share it, and buy again.

Now we come to the third part of your chapter request: how I grow a loyal circle that spreads a book by word of mouth.

This is where the real power lives. Advertising is expensive. Attention is unstable. Word of mouth is the strongest marketing because it travels on trust.

But word of mouth does not happen by begging people to "share." It happens when three things are true.

The book delivers.
The buyer feels respected.
The community feels involved.

If the book delivers, readers talk because they want others to benefit. They also talk because talking makes them look wise. People enjoy being the one who introduces a good resource.

If the buyer feels respected, they talk because they want to support a person who treats them well. Respect is a business strategy. Rudeness, delays, and careless delivery kill referrals faster than any competitor.

If the community feels involved, they talk because they feel ownership. They feel part of something bigger than a transaction.

So I build a loyal circle intentionally.

I start with a small founding group. I do not chase the crowd first. I choose a few people who are serious. They might be teachers, youth leaders, office workers, church leaders, or community organizers. I give them early access or a special signed copy. I ask them one simple question after they read: what part helped you most? Their answer teaches me how to market honestly. It also shows them that I value their experience.

Then I give them a role. Not a fake title, a real role. I might ask them to host a small gathering. I might ask them to introduce the book in their circle. I might ask them to recommend it to one person who needs it. Small roles create movement. Movement creates visibility.

I also protect their trust by being consistent. If I say I will deliver books on Friday, I deliver on Friday. If I say there will be a follow-up session, I show up. Consistency is the quiet language of credibility.

Sometimes envy tries to poison this stage. People may say, "Why are you doing this?" or "Who do you think you are?" I do not argue. I build quietly. A loyal circle is not built through debate. It is built through service.

Let me show you a simple story example that captures how word of mouth begins.

A teacher buys a book because she attended a short session. She uses one method in class. Students improve. Another teacher asks, "What did you use?" She shows the book. That second teacher buys. Now two teachers are talking. The book is no longer just my book. It is their tool. That is what you want. You want the book to become part of other people's solutions.

Another example.

A church youth leader buys copies for a small group because the book speaks about discipline and purpose. The group discusses it weekly. One youth changes a habit, and his friend notices. The friend asks, "What happened?" He says, "We are reading this book together." That friend joins. Now the book is spreading without me chasing anyone.

Word of mouth is not magic. It is the natural result of usefulness inside community.

Now, I want to speak honestly about the challenge of weak reading environments. Sometimes people want the results but they do not want to read. They want you to summarize everything in a few minutes. They want the fruit without planting.

I do not fight them with anger. I design around reality.

I use short sessions that make reading feel achievable.
I write in clear language that does not punish the reader.
I use story so the pages turn naturally.
I break the book into chapters that feel like steps.
I invite group reading so the burden is shared.

This is not lowering standards. This is building access.

As you build readers, you also build your identity. People begin to know you as a person who brings value. That identity matters. In weak markets, people often buy the person before they buy the product. Trust is personal. When your name becomes linked to clarity and service, your next book sells faster than your first, because you are no longer a stranger.

So what is the practical plan I follow, week after week, to build readers before I push books?

I choose one place.
I choose one lesson.
I choose one small gathering.
I invite a small group.
I teach.
I offer the book.
I follow up.

Then I repeat.

Not with pressure. With patience.

The work is slow at first, then it becomes steady.

At the end of this chapter, I want you to take a quiet moment and answer these questions as if you are planning a real business, not a dream.

Where do people already gather around you?
Is it a school, a church, an office, a club, a neighborhood group, a café circle, a youth meeting, or a women's association?

What problem do they already talk about?
Is it discipline, money, parenting, study struggles, leadership, relationships, identity, or survival?

What is one lesson from your book that can help them in twenty minutes?
Not the whole book. One strong piece.

Who are the first ten people you can invite to a small session?
Real names. Real faces.

What is the simplest way they can buy after the session?
Clear price. Clear payment. Clear delivery.

If you can answer those questions, you are not only writing. You are building readers. And when you build readers, you do not have to push books like a desperate man. Your books begin to move the way good things move, through trust, through usefulness, and through people who feel proud to share what helped them.

CHAPTER 5: WRITING WITH BUSINESS DISCIPLINE, NOT MOOD

When I first started writing seriously, I believed my biggest enemy was lack of talent. Later I learned my biggest enemy was mood. Mood is a beautiful visitor, but it is a terrible manager. Mood comes when it wants, leaves when it wants, and never pays rent. If you build your publishing life on mood, you will produce in bursts and disappear for long seasons. A burst can impress people. A steady rhythm builds a catalog. And a catalog is what turns books into a business.

The day I began to treat writing as business production, my relationship with the page changed. I stopped asking, "Do I feel like writing today?" and started asking, "What is the minimum I will produce today, even if today is heavy?" That question does not sound romantic, but it is the question that finishes books. It is the question that turns ideas into assets.

I learned this the hard way. I would have days when I felt sharp, and I wrote like a river. Then I would have days when life hit me, and I wrote nothing. When I returned after those gaps, the manuscript felt far away. I forgot the thread. The voice sounded unfamiliar. I started re-reading, re-planning, and re-doubting. That cycle is how books die. They do not die from one big failure. They die from repeated small stops.

So I built a finishing system. It has two pillars: a daily minimum and a weekly checkpoint. Those two tools sound simple, but they are strong enough to carry a serious author through unstable life.

The daily minimum is my promise to the book. It is the smallest amount of work that still counts as progress, even on the worst day. The point is not to impress anyone. The point is to protect momentum. If I keep touching the manuscript, the book stays warm. If the book stays warm, I can return tomorrow without starting from zero.

Here is what most writers do. They set a daily goal based on their best mood. They say, "I will write three thousand words every day." That can work for a week, then life shifts, and they break their promise. Once the promise is broken, shame enters. Shame makes you avoid the page. Avoidance creates distance. Distance creates fear. Fear makes you rewrite the beginning again and again because the middle feels too big. That is how mood wins.

My daily minimum is built for my worst mood, not my best mood. I choose a minimum that I can keep when power is unstable, when internet is weak, when travel disrupts me, when family issues press me, and when my mind feels tired. I do not choose a minimum that requires perfect conditions. I choose a minimum that survives real conditions.

Sometimes my daily minimum is a small number of words. Sometimes it is a set amount of time. Sometimes it is one section revised. The exact form does not matter as much as the discipline. What matters is that I keep the chain unbroken.

The daily minimum also does something else. It removes negotiation. If you negotiate with yourself every day, you will lose. Negotiation sounds wise, but it is often disguised delay. A daily minimum turns writing into a simple task, like washing your face. You do it because it is part of who you are, not because you are in a special mood.

Now, you might be thinking, "If the minimum is small, how do I finish a whole book?" This is where people misunderstand compounding. Small daily progress adds up faster than occasional big effort. A book is not finished by one heroic weekend. A book is finished by ordinary days stacked on top of each other.

I learned to treat writing like saving money. If you save a little consistently, you build a fund. If you only save when you feel rich, you stay broke. Writing works the same way. If you write only when you feel inspired, you stay unfinished. If you write a minimum even when you feel flat, you finish.

Let me show you how I use the weekly checkpoint, because the weekly checkpoint is what keeps the daily minimum from becoming random motion.

The weekly checkpoint is one fixed time each week when I review the manuscript like a publisher, not like an emotional artist. I check what I produced, what I learned, what slowed me down, and what I will do next. The weekly checkpoint is where I control drift. Without it, you can write every day and still end up with a messy book, because daily work without weekly direction can become a pile of pages that do not serve the promise.

During the weekly checkpoint, I ask myself simple questions.

Did I keep the daily minimum?
Did I move the draft forward or did I stay stuck polishing one chapter?
Which part of the manuscript is heavy right now, and why?
What is the next small target for the coming week?
Do I still honor the promise of the book, or am I drifting into side topics?

This weekly meeting with myself is where I act like a business owner checking operations. It is not an emotional ceremony. It is practical. It protects the book from becoming a private diary. It keeps the book aligned to the buyer, the promise, and the path to market.

Now I want to address the second part of this chapter: how I keep drafts moving without losing quality.

Some writers are afraid of speed because they believe speed produces shallow work. They confuse "drafting fast" with "publishing careless." Those are not the same. Drafting fast means you allow the book to exist. Publishing careless means you refuse to clean it. I draft with speed and revise with care. That separation is the heart of my method.

The first skill in keeping drafts moving is learning to write imperfectly on purpose.

This is painful for proud people, and I include myself in that group. A proud mind wants to sound perfect from the first paragraph. It wants every line to carry weight. But perfectionism is not quality. Perfectionism is often fear wearing a clean shirt.

When I draft, my only goal is clarity and completion. I am not trying to create final beauty. I am trying to put the full message on the table. I want the whole structure visible so I can improve it later. You cannot renovate a house that does not exist. You cannot polish a book that is still a fog.

So I give myself permission to write an ugly first draft. Ugly does not mean meaningless. Ugly means unfinished. Ugly means rough. Ugly means the book is still in work clothes. When I accept that, I write faster and I reduce inner resistance.

I also use a simple trick that saves me from stopping: placeholders.

When I reach a section I do not fully know yet, I do not stop the whole draft to research for hours. I write a short placeholder line that says what I intend to put there later. Then I continue. Stopping to research in the middle of drafting is like stopping a bus to polish the paint. The passengers are trying to reach a destination. Drafting is the journey to the destination. Editing is the paint.

Placeholders keep the bus moving.

Another way I keep drafts moving is by drafting in scenes and blocks rather than trying to write the whole chapter perfectly from beginning to end. Many writers get stuck because they force themselves to write in order even when their mind wants to jump. I allow myself to draft the easiest part of the chapter first, then fill gaps later. Momentum matters more than order during early drafting.

For example, if I know the closing story of a chapter but not the opening paragraph, I draft the closing story first. If

I know the practical lesson but not the example, I draft the lesson first. Then later I return and connect pieces. This method reduces friction, and friction is what slows production.

Now, about quality. I do not sacrifice quality. I postpone certain kinds of quality work until the right stage.

Quality has layers. There is structural quality, meaning the chapter order makes sense and the promise is delivered. There is clarity quality, meaning the reader understands without confusion. There is language quality, meaning sentences flow and feel strong. There is technical quality, meaning spelling, grammar, formatting, and consistency.

In the drafting stage, I focus on structural quality and clarity quality. I leave language elegance and technical perfection for later passes. That is not laziness. That is stage discipline. When you mix stages, you slow down and you lose momentum.

Let me show you how this looks in real life with a teaching example.

Nyakor is writing a book for students. She begins Chapter 2 and wants the first paragraph to sound like a speech that will make students cry with motivation. She spends three hours rewriting one paragraph. She feels productive, but the chapter is still empty. At the end of the day, she is tired and discouraged. That is mood writing.

Now Nyakor uses the daily minimum and the finish-first method. She drafts the chapter with simple clarity: the problem, the method, the example, the student action step, the recap. The paragraphs are not yet polished, but the chapter exists. At the weekly checkpoint, she sees she drafted two chapters in one week, and she feels real progress. That is business discipline.

Later, during revision, she can make the opening paragraph more powerful. But she will be editing a real chapter, not fighting emptiness.

This is the difference.

Now I will give you my "finish-first, polish-later" method in full, because this is the method that protects momentum and prevents the book from becoming a forever project.

Finish-first means I separate the work into clear phases.

First phase: draft to completion.
In this phase, I do not aim for beauty. I aim for a complete manuscript that follows the promise and covers every chapter. I allow rough sections and placeholders. I keep moving. The goal is to reach the last page.

Second phase: revise for structure and clarity.
Now that the manuscript exists, I read it like a reader. I cut repetition. I tighten chapters. I move sections to the right place. I add missing steps. I remove side topics that do not serve the promise. I make the logic clean. This is where the book becomes coherent.

Third phase: polish language.
Here I focus on sentence strength, rhythm, tone consistency, and removing unnecessary words. I do not turn this into perfection worship. I polish until the reading experience feels professional and clear.

Fourth phase: proof and technical cleanup.
This is where spelling, grammar, formatting consistency, headings, and layout issues are corrected. This phase prevents embarrassing errors from reaching the buyer.

Fifth phase: packaging and publishing preparation.
Cover, description, metadata, printing plan, platform files, proof copies, and launch plan. This is where the business side fully joins the writing.

When you respect these phases, you reduce chaos. You stop trying to do everything at once. And when you stop doing everything at once, your speed improves and your quality improves.

Now let me talk about momentum, because momentum is the real currency here.

Momentum is the feeling that the book is moving forward. When momentum is alive, writing feels lighter. When momentum dies, writing feels like pushing a car with no fuel.

Momentum is protected by two things: the daily minimum and short targets.

Short targets mean I do not tell myself, "I must finish the whole book." That target is too big for the mind. The mind will rebel. Instead, I tell myself, "Today I will complete this section," or "This week I will draft this chapter," or "This weekend I will finish the conclusion." Small targets create wins. Wins create energy. Energy protects momentum.

I also protect momentum by keeping a simple capture habit for ideas. Many writers lose momentum because they forget good lines and then feel the manuscript is weak. I capture ideas quickly when they come. A note on my phone. A short voice note. A sentence in a notebook. Later, during drafting, I can pull from that store. This reduces the feeling of emptiness and speeds drafting.

Now, I want to address a common fear: "If I draft fast, my book will be low quality and people will criticize me."

The real reason people criticize books is not that the author drafted fast. People criticize because the book does not deliver its promise, or because it is confusing, or because it looks careless. Those are revision and packaging failures, not drafting speed issues.

In fact, drafting slow can produce low quality too, because the author loses the thread and starts rewriting the beginning with no end. A book that never finishes has zero quality in the market because it does not exist. Completion is the first quality requirement.

This is why finish-first protects quality. It ensures the book exists. Then revision makes it strong.

I also want to speak to the writer who has unstable life conditions, because many writing systems assume perfect peace. I do not build systems for perfect peace. I build systems for real life.

Real life includes interruptions.
Real life includes travel.
Real life includes noise.

Real life includes emotional seasons.
Real life includes financial pressure.

The daily minimum is designed for real life. If you have only twenty minutes, the minimum fits. If you have no electricity, the minimum can be drafted by hand in a notebook. If you have a phone but no internet, the minimum can be typed offline. If you are tired, the minimum can be a rough paragraph that keeps the chain unbroken.

A serious author does not wait for perfect conditions. A serious author builds under constraints.

Now let me show you how I keep quality from slipping while I push drafts forward.

I use a simple internal rule: every chapter must answer one central question.

If the chapter is about "daily minimum," it must answer how to choose it, why it works, and how to apply it. If it starts drifting into ten other topics, the chapter becomes fog. Fog bores readers. Fog reduces referrals. A publisher removes fog.

So while drafting, I keep asking: what is the one central question of this chapter, and did I answer it clearly?

I also use what I call the "reader test" during revision. I imagine a real buyer, not a theoretical audience.

If the buyer is a busy worker, would they understand and apply this?
If the buyer is a student, would they feel guided or

lectured?

If the buyer is a leader, would they see steps or only opinions?

This test forces clarity. Clarity sells better than cleverness.

Now, let me take you into the emotional battlefield that ruins many authors: the middle of the book.

The beginning feels exciting because the idea is fresh. The end feels exciting because completion is near. The middle feels like work. The middle is where mood writers die.

Business discipline writers survive the middle because they do not rely on excitement. They rely on the daily minimum and weekly checkpoint.

When I hit the middle and feel bored, I do not panic. I do not assume the book is bad. I simply return to my system. I write the minimum. I keep going. Boredom is not a sign to stop. Boredom is often a sign that the book is becoming normal work, and normal work is where finished books come from.

I also handle doubt with a simple rule: doubts go into a separate note, not into the draft.

If I start arguing with myself inside the manuscript, the draft slows. So I keep a "doubt note" where I park questions like, "Is this chapter too long?" or "Do I need another example?" Then at the weekly checkpoint, I review those doubts calmly. Many doubts disappear when you see actual progress. Some doubts reveal useful edits. Either way, the draft keeps moving.

Now let me give you a practical picture of how a week can look when you apply this chapter.

During the week, I write my daily minimum. Sometimes it is small. Some days it becomes bigger because once I start, I keep going. But I never demand big. I only demand the minimum.

Then one day each week, I do the checkpoint. I look at what I produced. I choose the next chapter target. I identify what slowed me down. I prepare the next week's writing sessions by making the next step clear.

This is how a book becomes a predictable output, not a mysterious event.

And because this is a book business guide, let me connect discipline to money, because that link is what makes this chapter serious.

Every finished book is an asset.
Every unfinished book is a cost.

An unfinished book costs time.
It costs attention.
It costs emotional energy.
It costs opportunity because you could have been building the next asset.

A finished book can be packaged and sold.
It can earn.
It can lead to referrals.
It can become part of a catalog.

So when I choose discipline over mood, I am not only becoming a better writer. I am becoming a better business operator. I am building assets the way a farmer builds harvest.

Now I want to close with a clear teaching note for you, because I do not want you to admire this chapter and do nothing.

Choose your daily minimum today. Make it small enough to survive your worst day, not your best day.

Choose your weekly checkpoint time today. Fix it like an appointment.

Then adopt the finish-first, polish-later method. Promise yourself you will not polish the paint while the house is still half-built. Build the house first. Then polish it.

If you do this, you will finish more books.
If you finish more books, you will build a catalog.
If you build a catalog, you will reduce pressure on any single book.
And when pressure reduces, writing becomes calmer, marketing becomes easier, and your book business becomes steady instead of emotional.

That is writing with business discipline, not mood.

CHAPTER 6: STORY CRAFT THAT SELLS WITHOUT BEGGING

When people hear "book business," they often imagine spreadsheets, prices, ads, and distribution routes. Those things matter. But there is another engine that quietly determines whether a book sells again and again without you chasing buyers. That engine is story craft. If your pages do not hold attention, your marketing becomes a struggle. If your pages hold attention, your marketing becomes lighter, because the book creates its own advocates.

I learned this through experience, not theory. I have watched two books with similar topics perform very differently. One book sold a few copies, then died. The other book kept moving from hand to hand. The difference was not only the topic. The difference was the reading experience. People finish books that keep them turning pages. People recommend books that give them a satisfying payoff. And recommendations are the cleanest marketing in the world.

This chapter is about story craft that sells without begging. Not story craft for entertainment only, but story craft as a delivery system for lessons. In this book, I am the teacher, guide, and narrator. The characters I use are examples, not idols. They are living illustrations. They exist to carry a point into the reader's mind in a way that sticks.

Now, let me tell you the truth. Many nonfiction writers fear story. They think story makes the book less "serious." They think lessons must be delivered like a lecture to be respected. But readers are not classrooms. Readers are humans. Humans remember stories more than they remember abstract statements. Humans trust lessons that feel lived. Humans refer books that made them feel something and taught them something.

So I use story and clear lessons to keep pages turning.

This is the balance: story carries the lesson, and the lesson gives the story purpose.

If you write only story with no lesson, you might entertain, but you may not create outcomes. If you write only lesson with no story, you might inform, but many readers will not finish. A book business needs readers who finish, because finishers become promoters.

Here is the structure I use again and again.

I open with a real human situation.
I let the reader feel the problem.
I show the cost of staying stuck.
I introduce a decision or a method.
I show the shift.
I extract the lesson clearly.
I give the reader an action step or a clear takeaway.

That is my rhythm. It is simple, but it is powerful.

Now I will show you how I keep pages turning using story and clear lessons, starting with what I call the "pull."

The pull is the reason a reader continues from one page to the next. If there is no pull, the reader closes the book. And when the reader closes the book, it is very hard to bring them back.

Pull comes from three sources.

Curiosity: the reader wants to know what happens next.
Relevance: the reader feels, "This is about me."
Momentum: the writing moves without heavy fog.

Curiosity is created through questions and uncertainty. It does not require drama. It requires an unfinished tension. It can be as small as, "Will I solve this?" or as big as, "Will this decision destroy my future?"

Relevance is created when the situation mirrors the reader's life. The reader sees themselves inside the story. They think, "I have done that," or "I have felt that," or "I am afraid of that."

Momentum is created through clarity and pacing. You do not stop the story every two lines to explain theory. You let the story breathe, then you deliver the lesson in a clean moment.

This is why I say story craft sells without begging. A book that pulls readers forward does not need you to shout. It needs you to be consistent and present, and it will do the rest through referrals.

Now, the second part of this chapter: how I use characters only as teaching examples to drive a point home.

In my writing, characters serve a purpose. They are not there to show off my imagination. They are not there to confuse the reader with unnecessary detail. They are there to represent real reader types, real buyer concerns, and real life moments that shape decisions.

I use characters in three ways.

As mirrors.
A character reflects the reader's struggle.

As models.
A character demonstrates the method working in real life.

As warnings.
A character shows what happens when you ignore the lesson.

When I introduce Nyakor, she is a mirror for students and educators, and also a model for disciplined learning. When I introduce Mr. Aldridge, he is a model for leadership decisions and a warning against lazy management. When I introduce Mama Ajok, she is a mirror for practical survival concerns and a reminder that buyers do not live in abstract worlds.

Each character is selected to carry one clear teaching point. If the character does not serve a point, the character does not belong.

This is important because many writers confuse depth with complexity. They add many characters, many names, many side stories, and the reader gets lost. Lost readers do not finish. Unfinished books do not get referrals.

I prefer fewer characters and sharper purpose.

Now, how do I craft scenes with characters that carry lessons without becoming boring lectures?

I focus on what I call "decision moments."

A decision moment is when a character must choose between two paths.
One path leads to growth.
The other path leads to the same pain.

Readers love decision moments because decision is where life is. They see themselves. They also learn without feeling taught.

Let me show you a decision moment.

Nyakor is a teacher who wants her students to improve. She can either keep complaining about the system, or she can create a small reading circle and teach one method weekly. She chooses the reading circle. The story shows her resistance, her doubts, the first small success, then the shift in her students. That scene carries a lesson: change begins small and consistent. I can then state the lesson clearly: build readers before you push books, build habits before you demand results.

The story makes the lesson feel earned, not preached.

Now, the third part of this chapter: clarity, tension, and payoff create trust and referrals.

Let us start with clarity, because clarity is the foundation.

Clarity means the reader understands what is happening, why it matters, and what to do with it.

Many authors believe complexity makes them look smart. But complexity often makes readers feel stupid, and readers do not recommend books that made them feel stupid. Readers recommend books that made them feel capable.

So I write with clarity as an act of respect.

Clarity is not only simple words. Clarity is clean structure. It is one idea per paragraph. It is clear transitions. It is examples that explain rather than decorate. It is avoiding unnecessary detours.

When you write clearly, you reduce reader fatigue. Fatigue is the enemy of completion.

Now tension.

Tension is often misunderstood. People think tension means violence, arguments, or dramatic conflict. That is one kind of tension, but it is not the only kind. Tension is simply the feeling that something matters and is not resolved yet.

In nonfiction, tension can be created through a problem that is not solved, a question that is not answered, a risk that is not addressed, or a decision that has consequences.

For example, in this book business journey, tension exists because the author has something to sell but faces weak reading culture, limited money, unstable systems, and social pressure. The question is, will he build a working system or remain stuck in applause?

That is tension. And tension pulls the reader forward.

So I create tension by showing the cost of failure.

If you do not track stock, you lose money.
If you do not package well, you lose trust.
If you rely on mood, you do not finish.
If you launch and disappear, your sales die.
If you write for applause, you remain invisible.

These are not threats. They are realities. When I show them through story, the reader feels urgency without being manipulated.

Then payoff.

Payoff is the reward the reader receives for staying with you. Payoff can be emotional or practical, but it must be real. It must answer the tension you created.

If you build tension around "How do I finish a book when life is unstable?" the payoff must be a working method, not a motivational speech.

If you build tension around "How do I sell books offline in a weak market?" the payoff must be a system of distribution, not vague encouragement.

Payoff builds trust.

When a reader experiences payoff, they feel safe in your hands. They believe the next chapter will also deliver. They keep reading. They finish. And when they finish, they recommend.

This is the business link. Payoff creates referrals, and referrals create sales without begging.

Now let me teach you the craft techniques I use to produce clarity, tension, and payoff in a practical way.

First technique: open with a hook that is human, not theoretical.

Instead of starting a chapter with definitions, I start with a moment. A moment in a classroom. A moment in a shop. A moment in a family conflict. A moment where a decision must be made. Then I expand into teaching. This makes the reader feel like they entered a living room, not a lecture hall.

Second technique: keep scenes tight.

A scene is not a movie. It is a focused slice. I include only what the reader needs to see the point. I do not drown the reader in background details. The reader's mind is not your storage room. Give them what they need.

Third technique: attach the lesson to the scene immediately.

After a scene, I state the lesson clearly. I do not assume the reader will guess. Some readers will guess, but many will not. Clarity means you help the reader carry the lesson out of the story.

I often use a simple phrasing.

Here is what that taught me.
Here is the rule I extracted.
Here is the mistake to avoid.
Here is the step you can take this week.

Fourth technique: use repetition wisely.

People learn through repetition, but repetition must feel useful, not lazy. I repeat key ideas in different angles. I reinforce the same principle with different examples. This makes the book feel cohesive and strong, rather than scattered.

Fifth technique: end chapters with an action step.

Action steps create payoff and also create outcomes. A reader who applies your book gets results. A reader who gets results becomes a promoter. This is why action steps are not optional in a book business guide. They are referral machines.

Now, let me speak about something that many writers ignore: the emotional experience of the reader.

A reader buys a book with hope. They hope the book will help them. If your writing makes them feel judged, they resist. If your writing makes them feel seen, they open up. If your writing makes them feel guided, they trust. Trust is what creates referrals.

So I do not write as if I am above the reader. I write as a guide who has walked some distance ahead and is turning back to point at the safe path.

That is why first-person teaching is powerful. It feels like companionship. It also allows me to show my mistakes and the lessons that came from them. Readers do not trust a teacher who pretends to be perfect. They trust a teacher who is honest and still disciplined.

Now, I want to show you a short story pattern I use repeatedly, because it is one of the simplest ways to build trust.

I call it the "before, turning point, after" pattern.

Before: I describe the old mindset or struggle.
Turning point: I show the moment I realized the truth.
After: I show the new method and results.

This pattern creates emotional payoff and practical payoff. It also gives the reader hope because they see transformation is possible.

For example, before I understood business discipline, I wrote when I felt like it. Turning point: I realized mood was ruining me. After: I built a daily minimum and weekly checkpoint and finished more books. That is a transformation story. It teaches without preaching.

Now, let me tie this to the business result again, because this chapter must serve the bigger purpose of the book.

Books sell without begging when readers become your marketers.

Readers become your marketers when:

They finish the book.
They feel proud of what they learned.
They feel the book respected them.
They feel the book delivered.
They feel the book gave them language to explain it to others.

Story craft increases finishing.
Clear lessons increase pride and application.
Clarity reduces fatigue.
Tension keeps pages turning.
Payoff creates satisfaction.
Satisfaction produces referrals.

That chain is not theory. It is the logic of human behavior.

A person rarely recommends a book they did not finish.
A person rarely recommends a book that bored them.
A person rarely recommends a book that confused them.
A person eagerly recommends a book that helped them.

So if you want books as a business, you cannot ignore craft. Craft is not luxury. Craft is conversion.

Before I close, let me give you a practical exercise to apply this chapter to your own writing.

Choose one lesson your book teaches.
Now create one teaching scene around it.

Pick one character type that represents your buyer.
Place them in a real situation where the lesson matters.
Show the decision they face.
Show the consequence of the wrong choice.
Show the method or principle that solves it.
End with a clear takeaway and one action step.

Do this for three lessons, and you will have the skeleton of a book that keeps pages turning while still teaching clearly.

And remember the rule I live by as a publisher-writer.

Your story is not there to decorate your lesson.
Your story is there to deliver your lesson.

When you write like that, the reader feels carried.
When the reader feels carried, they finish.
When they finish, they talk.
When they talk, your book moves.

That is story craft that sells without begging.

CHAPTER 7: PACKAGING THE BOOK LIKE A PRODUCT PEOPLE CAN TRUST

The day I understood packaging, I stopped calling it "design stuff." I stopped treating it like decoration that can wait until I feel rich. I realized packaging is not makeup for a weak book. Packaging is the public proof that I respect the buyer. And in the book business, respect is what earns trust.

When a person sees your book for the first time, they do not know you. They do not know your sacrifice, your late nights, your sincerity, or your message. They only know what your book looks like, what it promises, and how safe it feels to spend money on it. In that moment, packaging is doing the talking for you.

This is why packaging is not a side task. Packaging is part of the product. It is the bridge between your value and the buyer's confidence.

I learned that in a painful way. I once had a book with strong teaching inside, but the cover looked like a rushed school project. The title was long and unclear. The subtitle tried to say everything and ended up saying nothing. The interior layout was tight and uncomfortable to read. People who opened it felt tired before they reached the first lesson. Some praised the idea, but fewer bought. And those who bought did not recommend it quickly, because they did not feel proud to hand it to someone else.

That is when I accepted a hard truth. In the market, buyers judge with their eyes before they judge with their minds. That does not mean people are shallow. It means people are cautious. Money is hard to earn, and trust is hard to give. A buyer must feel safe.

So I began packaging the book like a product people can trust.

A professional cover, title, subtitle, and interior layout

Let me begin with the cover, because the cover is your first salesperson.

A professional cover does three jobs fast.

It tells the buyer what the book is.
It tells the buyer who the book is for.
It tells the buyer what result or experience they will get.

If the cover fails at those three jobs, you can have the best writing in the world and still struggle, because most buyers will never open the book to discover your brilliance.

A professional cover is not only about beauty. It is about signal.

Your cover must signal genre and purpose.

If your book is a practical guide, the cover should feel clean, confident, and straightforward. The buyer should feel, "This will teach me something useful."

If your book is story-led nonfiction, the cover should feel human and emotionally grounded. The buyer should feel, "This will carry me through a real journey and leave me with meaning."

If your book is academic or serious reference, the cover should feel structured and calm. The buyer should feel, "This is credible and organized."

Many authors make a mistake here. They choose a cover style they personally like, instead of a cover style that matches what the buyer expects. When expectation and signal do not match, the buyer hesitates. Hesitation kills sales.

A professional cover also respects typography. Typography is not a fancy word. It simply means the style and clarity of the text.

A strong cover title must be readable at small size. Most online buyers see your cover as a tiny thumbnail. If the title is hard to read, the buyer scrolls past. In offline markets, the cover must still read clearly from a short distance on a table. If the title is thin, pale, or crowded, the book looks weak, even if the message is strong.

So I prioritize bold, clear, confident text. I avoid clutter. I avoid too many fonts. I avoid decorative confusion. A book cover is not a place to show every creative skill you have. It is a place to make one promise feel trustworthy.

Color matters too. Color carries emotion and genre signal. It also carries pricing signal. A cheap-looking color combination makes the book feel cheap. A calm, balanced palette makes the book feel professional. This is not about luxury. This is about perception.

Images and graphics must serve the message. If you use imagery, it should clarify the promise, not distract. A random picture may look nice, but it can confuse the buyer. Confusion is the enemy.

Now, let us talk about the title, because the title is often the biggest packaging mistake.

Many writers choose titles to sound clever. They want to impress. They want applause. But buyers do not pay for cleverness. Buyers pay for clarity.

A strong title is a clear doorway. It tells the buyer what world they are entering. It gives them language for their need. It makes them feel seen.

When I choose a title, I think like this.

If the buyer sees only the title, will they understand what this book does for them?

If the answer is no, I rewrite.

A title can be short, but it must not be vague. A title can be poetic, but it must still connect to a real promise. If the title is too abstract, you will spend your whole marketing life explaining what the book is. That is exhausting.

The subtitle is where I get practical. A subtitle is not a decoration. A subtitle is the promise in plain language.

A good subtitle usually answers some combination of these:

Who the book is for.
What result it provides.
How it provides that result, in simple terms.
What pain it helps the reader avoid.

When the subtitle does its job, the buyer stops guessing.

Now the interior layout, because this is where trust becomes physical.

Many authors think layout does not matter. They think, "As long as the words are there, it is fine." But the reader's eyes and mind live inside the layout. If the layout is uncomfortable, reading becomes work. When reading becomes work, readers quit. When readers quit, referrals shrink.

A professional interior layout is quiet. It does not call attention to itself. It supports the reader.

Spacing matters. If the lines are too tight, the page feels heavy. If margins are too narrow, the book feels cramped. If font size is too small, readers feel punished. If the font style is strange, readers feel distracted.

Chapter starts should feel intentional. Headings should be consistent. Page numbers should be clean. The table of contents should be accurate. The overall experience should feel stable from the first page to the last.

I do not treat this as perfection worship. I treat it as buyer respect.

When a reader feels comfortable, they keep going. When they keep going, they finish. When they finish, they recommend. That is business logic hiding inside layout.

How design affects pricing power and credibility

Pricing is not only math. Pricing is also belief. Buyers ask a silent question when they see a price.

Is this worth it?

Design helps them answer that question in your favor.

If your cover looks cheap, the buyer expects a cheap price. If you try to price it higher, they resist. Not because they hate you, but because the signal and price do not match.

If your cover looks professional, the buyer accepts a higher price more easily, because the product feels like it belongs at that level.

This is why good design creates pricing power. Pricing power means you are not forced to sell low to survive. You can charge fairly for the value you deliver, and still have buyers who feel good about buying.

Credibility is also tied to design. In the real world, people use visual cues as shortcuts for trust.

A school administrator deciding whether to buy 100 copies for students will judge your book in seconds. If the book looks unprofessional, they worry it will embarrass them. They also worry about content quality, even if the content is strong, because they cannot test every page.

A pastor or church leader considering a bulk order will also judge the book by how it feels in hand. If the book looks careless, they hesitate to recommend it publicly.

An office manager will not place a weak-looking book on a conference table, even if the topic is needed. Image matters in professional spaces.

This is why packaging is not vanity. Packaging is credibility.

There is another side of pricing power too. Good packaging reduces returns and complaints. When buyers know what they are getting, and the book looks and feels professional, fewer people feel tricked. Fewer people request refunds or refuse to pay. Trust reduces friction.

In offline markets, good packaging also reduces haggling. People haggle more when the product looks weak. They feel they can push you down. When the book looks solid, the price feels more fixed, like a real product in a shop.

So design does not only help you sell. It helps you hold your price with dignity.

How I position the book so the buyer knows exactly what they get

Positioning is where many authors fail quietly. They package the book nicely, but the buyer still does not understand the offer. The title says one thing. The cover design suggests another. The description says something else. The buyer becomes unsure.

Uncertainty makes people delay. Delay kills sales.

Positioning means alignment. The promise must match across the whole product.

The cover promise.
The title and subtitle promise.
The back cover or description promise.
The chapter structure promise.

Everything should point to the same outcome.

This is where the promise statement from Chapter 3 becomes a tool, not a theory. I use the promise statement as my alignment test.

If the promise is "a step-by-step guide to selling books offline and online," then the cover must look like a practical guide, not like a romance novel. The title must speak clearly to publishing and selling, not to abstract "dreams." The subtitle must tell the buyer what is inside, not just flatter the author. The interior layout must support step-by-step teaching, not long cramped paragraphs that feel like a sermon.

If the promise is story-led, then the cover should not look like a textbook. The typography and imagery should suggest a real journey, not a manual. The description should not read like a business brochure. It should read like an invitation to experience and learn.

Positioning is also about who you are refusing to serve.

This sounds harsh, but it is freeing. If you try to position your book for everyone, your message becomes soft. A buyer wants to feel the book is written for them. That feeling comes when you choose.

So I position with sharp buyer clarity.

I speak directly to the buyer type. I use the buyer's language. I name the problem the way the buyer names it. I do not hide behind poetic language when the buyer wants a solution. And I do not hide behind dry language when the buyer wants a story that carries truth.

In offline settings, positioning must be even clearer, because people may not be used to browsing books and reading long descriptions. The cover and short pitch must do most of the work.

When I present a book at a small gathering, I say the promise in one breath.

This book is for you if you are trying to do this.
It will help you do that.
Here is how it does it.
Here is what you will walk away with.

That pitch should match the cover. If my pitch sounds different from my packaging, trust cracks.

Now I will make this chapter more practical by walking through the parts of packaging the way I operate as a publisher.

I begin with the buyer's first impression.

What does the buyer see first, online or offline?

Online, the buyer sees a thumbnail. So I check thumbnail readability. Can the title be read on a phone? Does the cover look clean at small size? Does the image become messy when shrunk? Are the colors muddy? Does the design look crowded?

Offline, the buyer sees the physical object. So I check physical presence. Does the cover feel sturdy? Does the finish look professional? Does the spine read clearly on a shelf? Does the back cover help a buyer decide quickly? Is the print quality clean?

Then I move to promise clarity.

If someone reads only the title and subtitle, do they know what they get?

If someone reads only the first few lines of the description, do they understand the offer?

If someone flips through the table of contents, do they see a clear journey?

If the answer is no, I fix it before I publish or print in volume.

Then I look at internal trust signals.

Do my chapter headings feel organized?
Does the table of contents match the chapters?
Is the font comfortable?
Is the spacing readable?
Are there obvious errors that signal carelessness?

A single careless error can poison trust, especially in skeptical markets. People may forgive an error, but they will still judge your seriousness.

Now I want to talk about a very practical part of packaging that many authors ignore, especially in offline markets.

The back cover and the inside first pages.

The back cover is often the closest thing you have to a salesperson in a shop. If your book sits on a table, a buyer picks it up, looks at the back, and decides in seconds.

So the back cover must be simple and strong.

It should name the problem.
State the promise.
Explain what the reader will learn or gain.
Show who the book is for.
Give a short credibility line about you, without bragging.
Provide clear price if you print it there, or at least clear contact and availability.

Inside the book, the first pages also matter. If those pages look messy, the buyer feels regret. If those pages look clean, the buyer feels relief.

This is why I keep front matter tidy, consistent, and purposeful. I do not overload it. I use it to set expectations, then I move into the content.

Now let us talk about "professional" in a grounded way, because sometimes people use that word to bully authors. Professional does not mean expensive. Professional means intentional.

A simple cover can be professional if it is clean, readable, and aligned to genre.
A basic interior can be professional if it is consistent, comfortable, and organized.
A short title can be professional if it is clear and buyer-focused.

Professional is not about showing off. Professional is about removing doubt.

That is what packaging does. It removes doubt.

Here is another truth that changed me. Packaging is also a filter. It filters out buyers who are not a fit, and it attracts buyers who are.

When your packaging is clear, the right buyers feel pulled. The wrong buyers feel uninterested. That is good. You do not want confused buyers who later complain, "This is not what I expected." Clear packaging reduces that pain.

Now let me bring the characters back in as teaching examples.

Imagine Mama Ajok in a market. She sees a book on a table. She will not read a long description. She will look at the title, the cover, maybe the back cover, and she will decide quickly. If the cover is crowded and unclear, she walks away. If the cover is calm and the promise is clear, she pauses. If the back cover tells her the book can solve a problem she feels, she buys. That is packaging doing the work.

Imagine Mr. Aldridge in an office. He sees a leadership book. If the cover looks amateur, he will not risk buying it for his team. If it looks credible, he feels safe. He might even buy multiple copies. That is packaging creating bulk opportunity.

Imagine Nyakor in a school. She wants resources that look respectable in front of students. If the cover looks like a casual flyer, she hesitates. If it looks like a serious educational tool, she becomes confident to recommend it. That is packaging creating trust that multiplies.

Now, a final part of packaging that many authors ignore is positioning the book inside a larger catalog.

When I build books as a business, I do not package each book as a lonely island. I package with pathways in mind. I make it clear what the next step is. I mention related books in the back matter. I keep a consistent visual identity across a series, so readers recognize the family.

Consistency builds brand trust. When someone sees your next book, they already feel familiar. Familiarity reduces selling friction.

But consistency must not become boredom. You can keep a recognizable style while still giving each book a distinct identity. The goal is that a reader can say, "This is a Panyim book," and also say, "This is the one that solves my specific problem."

That is brand clarity without confusion.

Let me close this chapter with the way I check packaging before I release a book, because I want you to leave with a working habit, not inspiration only.

I ask myself:

If I were a stranger, would I trust this cover?
If I saw this as a thumbnail, would I click?
If I saw this on a table, would I pick it up?
If I read the title and subtitle, would I understand the promise?
If I read the back cover or description, would I know exactly what I get?
If I opened the book, would the layout feel comfortable and serious?
If I paid this price, would I feel satisfied with the product quality?

If any answer is weak, I fix it before I scale.

Because once you print 500 copies or publish widely online, mistakes become expensive. Packaging mistakes do not only waste money. They waste time, reputation, and momentum.

And momentum is precious in the book business.

So remember this rule the next time you feel tempted to rush.

A manuscript is private value.
Packaging turns that value into a public product.
Public products must earn trust on first contact.

When you package your book like a product people can trust, you stop selling with pressure. You start selling with confidence. Buyers feel safe. They buy. They finish. They recommend. And the book begins to move in the world the way it was meant to move.

CHAPTER 8: THE MONEY MATH OF PUBLISHING

I used to treat money like an uncomfortable topic, as if talking about it would stain the purity of writing. Then I learned something that made me calmer. Money is not a stain. Money is a meter. It tells me whether my publishing system is healthy or leaking. It tells me whether a book can stand on its own feet or whether it keeps leaning on my pocket until I get tired and quit.

In the early days, I would print a small batch, sell a few copies, feel proud, then realize I had no clear idea what I actually earned. Sometimes I felt rich because cash came in, but later I discovered the cash was only replacing what I spent. Other times I felt discouraged because sales were slow, but if I had calculated properly, I would have seen that even slow sales were still profitable and worth continuing.

That is why I built a simple way of thinking about money. I do not need fancy accounting to start. I need plain language, clean records, and honesty with numbers. If my numbers are clean, my decisions become clean. If my numbers are dirty, my emotions take control.

So in this chapter I will teach pricing, margins, and break-even in plain language. I will show how I control printing costs, avoid waste, and plan inventory. Then I will explain how I reinvest profits to scale without debt pressure.

Let me start with the simplest truth in publishing.

A book business survives on the difference between what a copy costs me and what a copy brings in.

That difference is the space where profit lives, but only if I measure it properly.

There are two types of costs I watch.

One-time costs, which I pay once for the whole book. These include editing, cover design, formatting, ISBN if I buy it, initial proof copies, and sometimes marketing setup like a basic website page or print flyers.

Per-copy costs, which increase each time I print or ship a copy.

These include printing cost per unit, packaging materials, transport, delivery fees, and platform fees if I am selling online through a marketplace.

If I mix these two, I confuse myself. If I separate them, money becomes clear.

Now I will explain pricing.

Pricing is not simply picking a number that "feels fair." Pricing is choosing a number that covers costs, leaves a healthy margin, and matches what the buyer believes the book is worth.

When I choose a price, I think in two directions at once.

I look backward at my costs so I do not sell at a loss.
I look forward at the buyer's value so the price makes sense in the market.

If I only look at costs, I might price too high and reduce sales.

If I only look at buyers, I might price too low and trap myself in stress.

So I meet in the middle with math and common sense.

Let us define margin in plain language.

Margin is what remains after costs, and it is what gives me breathing room.

The simplest margin to understand is what I call per-copy profit from direct sales.

If it costs me 3 dollars to produce one copy, and I sell it directly for 10 dollars, my per-copy profit is 7 dollars.

But I must be careful. "Costs" must include everything that truly belongs to that sale. If I deliver the book and spend 1 dollar on transport per copy, the true per-copy cost is not 3 dollars. It is 4 dollars. Then the per-copy profit becomes 6 dollars.

When I calculate like this, I stop fooling myself.

Now I will show you break-even, because break-even is the turning point where a book stops being an expense and starts becoming a source of funds.

Break-even means I have earned back the one-time costs for that book.

Here is the simplest way to calculate break-even copies.

Break-even copies equal the one-time costs divided by the per-copy profit.

Let me walk through an example carefully, step by step.

Suppose my one-time costs for a book are 300 dollars. That 300 dollars might include editing and cover design and formatting.

Suppose my per-copy cost, including printing and average delivery, is 4 dollars.

Suppose I sell the book directly at gatherings for 10 dollars.

Per-copy profit is 10 dollars minus 4 dollars. That is 6 dollars.

Now break-even copies equal 300 dollars divided by 6 dollars per copy.

300 divided by 6 is 50.

So I break even after selling 50 copies.

After copy number 50, the per-copy profit is no longer paying back the one-time costs. It becomes profit I can reinvest or save.

This one calculation changes how you feel about publishing. If you know your break-even is 50 copies, you stop acting like every sale must be a miracle. You can plan calmly. You can set targets. You can build habits.

Now, life is not always direct sales. Many authors sell through partners, shops, schools, and organizations. That changes the per-copy profit because you may sell at a lower price to allow the partner to earn too.

This is where people get confused and end up making bad deals.

So I keep it simple. I think of different pricing lanes.

Direct price is the price when I sell to the reader myself.

Wholesale price is the price when I sell to a shop or an organization that will resell.

Consignment is not a price lane by itself, it is a payment arrangement. The shop sells at the retail price, keeps an agreed portion, and gives me the rest after the sale.

Let me show you with numbers again, because numbers remove confusion.

Suppose my per-copy cost is still 4 dollars.

If I sell directly at 10 dollars, per-copy profit is 6 dollars.

If I sell wholesale to a shop, the shop needs room to earn. If the shop sells at 10 dollars, maybe the shop wants 30 percent or 40 percent. That means I might sell the copy to the shop for 6 dollars or 7 dollars.

Let us pick 6.50 dollars as an example.

Per-copy profit at wholesale becomes 6.50 dollars minus 4 dollars.
That is 2.50 dollars.

Now my break-even copies change. If my one-time costs are still 300 dollars, break-even copies become 300 divided by 2.50.

To compute that, I do it in a clean way.
2.50 is the same as 250 cents.
300 dollars is 30,000 cents.
30,000 divided by 250 equals 120.

So at this wholesale margin, I break even after 120 copies.

That does not mean wholesale is bad. It simply means I must plan volume, or I must balance wholesale with direct sales.

This is why I like hybrid selling. Direct sales give me high margin. Wholesale gives me reach and volume. Together, they stabilize the business.

Now let us talk about the trap that destroys many authors.

They set a price based on what they personally can afford, not based on what the product requires.

If a book costs me 4 dollars to produce and deliver, and I price it at 5 dollars because I feel sorry for buyers, I leave only 1 dollar per copy. Then my break-even becomes painful. If the one-time costs are 300 dollars, break-even becomes 300 divided by 1, which is 300 copies. In a weak reading market, 300 copies might take too long. The author gets tired. The author stops. The book dies.

I am not saying we must be greedy. I am saying we must be honest. If the price cannot sustain the system, the system collapses, and then even the buyers lose because the author disappears.

So I price with sustainability.

Now let me show you how I control printing costs, avoid waste, and plan inventory, because printing is where many book businesses bleed quietly.

Printing cost is not one fixed thing. It is affected by choices.

Page count affects cost. More pages usually means higher cost.
Trim size affects cost. Some sizes are cheaper because they are common.
Paper type affects cost.
Color printing is usually far more expensive than black and white.
Binding type affects cost.
Print quantity affects cost because unit cost often drops as quantity rises, but only if you can actually sell the stock.

So I treat printing like a negotiation between three forces.

Quality the buyer expects.
Cost I must control.
Volume I can realistically sell.

This is where waste enters the picture.

Waste happens when I print too many copies based on hope rather than a sales plan.

Hope printing looks like this.
I print 1,000 copies because I want to feel like a big publisher.
Then I sell 120 copies in three months.
The remaining 880 copies sit, get damaged, get stolen, get damp, get outdated, or become a burden when I move houses or travel.
That stock is not "inventory." It is trapped money.

So I avoid waste by printing in rounds.

A round is a print batch that matches my sales speed and my cash capacity.

If I can sell 100 copies in a month through schools and gatherings, then printing 200 or 300 might be reasonable. If I can sell 20 copies in a month, then printing 500 is a trap.

I prefer to start with a smaller round, prove demand, then scale the next round.

Scaling is safer when demand is proven.

I also control costs by controlling revisions before big printing.

One of the most expensive wastes is printing a large batch, then discovering errors or needing to update content. Then you either sell defective copies and damage trust, or you discard copies and lose money.

So I proof seriously before large print runs. I do not rush that step. A single proof copy that reveals mistakes can save you from losing hundreds of dollars.

Now let me talk about inventory planning, because inventory is where discipline becomes visible.

Inventory is simply the number of copies you have and where they are.

If you do not track inventory, you will lose money. It is not a matter of "maybe." You will lose money.

So I track inventory in a simple way.

I track copies in hand.
I track copies placed with partners.
I track copies sold.
I track copies returned.
I track cash collected.
I track cash owed.

I do not need fancy software to start. A notebook works. A simple spreadsheet works. What matters is that I can answer basic questions quickly.

How many copies do I have right now?
Where are they?
How many sold this week?
How much money came in?
How much money is still owed?

If I cannot answer those questions, I am not running a business. I am carrying books.

Now, planning inventory also means deciding when to reprint, and this is where many authors wait too long.

They wait until they are completely out of stock.
Then they rush printing.
Then they lose sales during the printing delay.
Then they break trust with buyers who asked and could not get the book.

So I use a simple idea: a reorder point.

A reorder point is the number of copies at which I begin the reprint process.

The reorder point depends on two things.

How fast I sell, which is my sales speed.
How long printing takes, which is my lead time.

If I sell 10 copies per week and printing takes 2 weeks, and I want a safety cushion, my reorder point might be 30 copies. That way, I can keep selling while I print the next round.

If I sell 50 copies per week and printing takes 3 weeks, my reorder point must be higher.

This is not complicated. It is simply matching supply to real demand.

Now I will show you how I control costs in practical, human ways, not only in theory.

First, I choose design decisions that do not inflate printing unnecessarily.
For example, if I can teach the same lesson in 200 pages instead of 280 pages, I reduce cost and also improve reader completion. Many authors add pages to look

serious, but serious is not page count. Serious is usefulness.

Second, I standardize some production choices across my catalog.
If I keep a consistent trim size and similar paper choices for a series, I can predict costs better and negotiate better with local printers.

Third, I compare quotes and I ask the right questions.
I do not only ask, "What is the total price?"
I ask, "What is the unit price at this quantity?"
I ask, "What changes if I print 200 instead of 300?"
I ask, "What is the difference between this paper and that paper?"
I ask, "How much does cover finish affect cost?"
When I ask like this, I gain control.

Fourth, I reduce spoilage.
I store books properly. I protect from moisture. I use clean packaging for transport. I avoid leaving boxes in risky places. This sounds small, but small losses add up. A book damaged is money damaged.

Now we come to reinvesting profits, because profit is not only for spending. Profit is the fuel that scales a catalog.

Many authors make this mistake.
They sell 100 copies, receive cash, feel relief, then spend the money on emergencies and personal pressure. Then they cannot reprint. Then the business stops. They say, "Books do not work." In truth, books were working, but profit was not being managed.

So I built a reinvestment habit.

I treat book profit as business money first, personal money second.

This does not mean I do not live. It means I do not kill the engine that feeds me.

I reinvest in three directions.

I reinvest into production, meaning the next print run, better editing, better covers, and better formatting.

I reinvest into distribution, meaning transport, partnerships, placement, and reliable stock availability.

I reinvest into visibility, meaning small promotion activities that keep the book in front of people, like workshops, sample chapters, basic ads if I use them, or travel to key selling points.

I also keep a small reserve, because debt often comes from surprise costs. When your printer increases prices or your transport becomes expensive or your life throws a problem at you, a reserve prevents panic borrowing.

Now let me explain how I scale without debt pressure.

Debt pressure in publishing usually comes from printing too many copies with borrowed money, hoping sales will repay fast.

Sometimes that works, but it is risky, especially in markets where sales can be slow or inconsistent.

I prefer scaling with a stair-step method.

I print a round that I can afford.
I sell through it.
I use part of the profit to fund the next round.
I increase quantity gradually as demand proves itself.
I keep my reorder point so I never run dry.
I build a catalog so no single title carries the whole weight.

This method is slower than gambling, but it is safer. It protects my peace. It also protects my family and my mission from the stress of chasing repayments.

Here is how it looks in a story example.

Imagine I print 200 copies of a book.
My per-copy cost is 4 dollars, so printing cost for 200 is 800 dollars.
I sell them at a direct price of 10 dollars.

Total revenue if I sell all 200 is 2,000 dollars.
Total variable costs already paid are 800 dollars, but remember I also have one-time costs, say 300 dollars.

So total costs are 800 plus 300, which is 1,100 dollars.
Profit after selling all 200 becomes 2,000 minus 1,100, which is 900 dollars.

Now I do not treat the 900 like free money.
I decide what portion funds the next print run.
If I want to print 300 copies next, I estimate the cost.
If the per-copy cost remains 4 dollars, 300 copies cost 1,200 dollars.

My profit is 900, which is not enough to print 300 without adding more cash.
So I can either print 200 again, which costs 800, and keep

the cycle moving without debt, or I can adjust by increasing the price slightly if the market allows, or I can add a bulk deal with an organization to create a larger cash inflow safely.

This is how scaling becomes a planning exercise, not a panic exercise.

Debt pressure comes when people scale faster than their cash can support.

I avoid that by matching print size to proven demand and cash reality.

Now let me talk about a quiet part of reinvestment that many authors ignore.

Reinvesting also means improving the product based on feedback.

If readers consistently struggle with one chapter, I revise it before the next print run.
If a cover is not converting, I improve it.
If the title is unclear and buyers keep asking, "What is it about?" I sharpen the subtitle.
These improvements are reinvestments because they increase future sales without increasing your workload.

A better package increases pricing power.
A clearer promise increases conversion.
A cleaner layout increases completion.
Higher completion increases referrals.

So reinvestment is not only printing more copies.
Reinvesment is also making the existing copy sell better.

Now I want to speak directly about avoiding waste, because waste is not only paper damage or unsold stock. Waste is also selling time.

If I do not know my numbers, I waste time chasing activities that do not pay.

For example, if I do ten events that each sell two copies, that is twenty copies. If the travel and time are heavy, maybe the net profit is small. If I do one school partnership that sells fifty copies in one order, that is more efficient.

This is why money math is not cold. Money math is time protection.

It helps me choose what to repeat and what to stop.

Now I will close this chapter by giving you a simple way to set up your own money math for one book, without turning you into an accountant.

Start with one-time costs.
Write them down clearly.

Then calculate per-copy cost.
Include printing.
Include average delivery or transport.
Include packaging materials.
Include any platform fees if selling online, or at least estimate them.

Then decide your price lanes.
Decide your direct price.
Decide your wholesale or partner price if you will use one.

Make sure each lane still leaves a profit after per-copy costs.

Then calculate break-even for each lane.
One-time costs divided by per-copy profit.

Then decide your print round.
Choose a quantity you can afford and realistically sell in a reasonable time.

Then set your reorder point.
Base it on sales speed and printing lead time.

Then set your reinvestment rule.
Decide in advance that a portion of profit returns to printing and growth before personal spending.

When you do these things, publishing stops being a guessing game. It becomes a system you can trust.

And that is what I want for you, because books as a business is not only about writing. It is about staying in the game long enough for your catalog to mature.

Money math is the discipline that keeps you in the game without begging, without panic, and without debt that steals your sleep.

CHAPTER 9: PUBLISHING ROUTES AND THE TRADEOFFS I REFUSE TO IGNORE

When I became serious about books as a business, I stopped asking the lazy question, "Where can I publish?" and started asking the harder question, "Which route fits this book, this market, and this season of my life without trapping me?" That shift saved me from many mistakes.

Publishing is not one road. It is a set of routes, and each route has tradeoffs. Some tradeoffs are obvious, like cost and speed. Some tradeoffs are hidden, like rights, control, and long-term flexibility. Many authors ignore those hidden tradeoffs, then wake up later trapped in a deal they cannot reverse.

In this chapter, I will teach the differences between local printing, self-publishing platforms, and partnerships. I will show what rights matter and what mistakes trap authors in bad deals. Then I will give you my checklist for choosing the best route for each book.

I refuse to ignore tradeoffs because tradeoffs are where freedom is won or lost.

The three main routes

Let me define the three routes in plain language.

Local printing means I produce printed copies through a local printer or print shop. I hold physical stock. I distribute and sell through my own channels or through local partners like shops, schools, churches, offices, and events.

Self-publishing platforms means I publish through online services that list the book on marketplaces, and may also print on demand. This includes ebooks, paperbacks, and sometimes hardcovers. The platform handles parts of production and distribution, but I still control the publishing decisions if I do it right.

Partnerships means I work with another party who helps with printing, distribution, marketing, or funding, in exchange for some share of revenue, rights, or control. Partnerships can be with a traditional publisher, a hybrid publisher, a sponsor organization, a bookstore chain, a printing company offering financing, or even a friend with money.

All three routes can work. None is perfect. The point is not to choose one route forever. The point is to choose the best route for each book, based on your buyer, your market, your cash position, your skills, and your long-term plan.

Route 1: Local printing

Local printing is the oldest route and still one of the most powerful, especially in markets where online buying is weak, where shipping is unreliable, or where readers prefer physical books.

The strengths of local printing are clear.

Speed to physical copies can be fast if the printer is reliable.

Unit cost can be controlled, especially if you print in volume.
Offline sales can bring cash quickly.
You can serve bulk buyers like schools and organizations directly.
You hold the stock, so you are not dependent on an online listing to exist.

But local printing has tradeoffs that many authors ignore.

First, inventory risk.
If you print too many copies, you trap money in boxes. If the book does not move fast, you carry that burden.

Second, quality control depends on the printer. Some printers are excellent. Some are careless. If you do not proof properly and monitor quality, you can end up with inconsistent batches, weak binding, faded covers, or wrong trimming.

Third, distribution becomes your job.
If you do not build channels, the books sit.

Fourth, your reach is limited by your physical movement. If you cannot travel or build partners, your sales remain local.

I still use local printing because it gives me control and cash flow. But I do not romanticize it. I treat it as a route that requires operational discipline: tracking stock, tracking money, managing storage, and building distribution.

Route 2: Self-publishing platforms

Self-publishing platforms changed the publishing world because they reduced gatekeeping. They allow an author to publish globally without asking permission. They also allow print-on-demand, meaning books can be printed per order, reducing inventory risk.

The strengths of self-publishing platforms include:

Global reach through marketplaces.
Print-on-demand reduces the need to hold stock.
Ebook distribution is fast and cheap.
Updates and revisions can be made more easily than in large local print runs.
Metadata tools allow discoverability if you understand buyer intent.

But platforms have tradeoffs too.

First, platform dependence.
If your book exists only on a platform and your account is suspended or your listing is blocked, you can lose sales suddenly.

Second, platform fees and royalty structures.
You do not keep the full retail price. The platform takes its portion, and printing costs are deducted.

Third, competition is intense.
You are listed beside many other books. If your packaging and positioning are weak, you become invisible.

Fourth, you must understand technical preparation.
Poor formatting, wrong files, or sloppy metadata can bury your book.

Fifth, you may not control the buyer relationship fully. On many marketplaces, you do not get the buyer's email or contact details, which limits direct follow-up.

I use self-publishing platforms because they are powerful for scaling and for building a catalog that sells while I sleep. But I manage the risks by also building direct sales channels and by maintaining backups of files and listings.

Route 3: Partnerships

Partnerships can accelerate a book business when done with clarity and integrity. They can also destroy a writer's freedom when done with desperation.

Partnerships come in many forms.

A traditional publisher may offer editing, cover design, printing, distribution, and marketing, but often requires rights and control.

A hybrid publisher may offer services for a fee while allowing the author to keep more rights, but the quality varies widely and some are simply expensive service providers.

A sponsor organization may fund printing for a book that supports their mission, then distribute copies in their networks.

A bookstore chain might partner for bulk orders or exclusive distribution.

A business partner might fund printing in exchange for a revenue share.

Partnerships can bring strengths:

Upfront funding reduces personal cash pressure.
Distribution networks can expand reach quickly.
Professional production support can improve quality.
Credibility can increase if the partner has a strong name.

But partnerships have tradeoffs:

You may lose control over pricing, cover, or messaging.
You may give up rights that are hard to regain.
Revenue shares can reduce profit.
Contracts can trap you if terms are unclear.
Partners may underperform and still hold your rights.

I do not reject partnerships. I reject blind partnerships. I refuse to ignore what is being exchanged.

Rights that matter

Now let me talk about rights, because rights are where authors get trapped.

Rights are simply permissions and controls over how the book can be used, produced, and sold.

The rights that matter most include:

Copyright ownership.
This is the basic ownership of the work. If you give up copyright, you give up the work itself.

Print rights.
Who has the right to produce and sell printed editions?

Ebook rights.
Who can produce and sell the digital edition?

Audio rights.
Who can produce and sell an audiobook?

Translation rights.
Who can translate and publish in other languages?

Territory rights.
Where can the book be sold? Local only? Regional? Global?

Term length.
For how long does the partner hold the rights? One year? Five years? Life of copyright?

Exclusivity.
Is the partner the only one allowed to publish and sell, or can you also sell elsewhere?

Derivative and adaptation rights.
Can the work be adapted into courses, workbooks, film, or other products?

Marketing and branding rights.
Can the partner alter the title, cover, or messaging?

Most authors who get trapped did not lose because they were stupid. They lost because they were eager. Eagerness makes you sign what you did not fully understand.

So I built a simple rule.

I do not sign away rights I do not fully understand.
I do not sign away rights I am not compensated for.
I do not sign away rights forever when I only need help for one season.

That rule keeps me free.

Common mistakes that trap authors

Now let me show you the mistakes I have seen and the traps I refuse to enter.

Mistake one: signing without clear revenue math. Some contracts promise "royalties," but the author never sees clear reporting or clear payment schedules. The author also does not calculate what their percentage means after costs. A contract that says "10 percent royalty" can sound like something, but if the base is small or costs are deducted first, the author may earn almost nothing.

Mistake two: giving exclusive rights with no performance requirement.
If a partner has exclusive rights but no obligation to produce, distribute, or market at a certain level, they can do nothing and still block you from doing something. This is one of the worst traps.

Mistake three: long contract terms with no exit clause.
If the term is five to ten years and there is no clean way to terminate based on underperformance, you are locked. Your book becomes a prisoner.

Mistake four: vague definitions of "net."
Many contracts pay royalties based on "net receipts." Net can be manipulated if the partner subtracts many costs

before calculating your share. If "net" is not clearly defined, you are exposed.

Mistake five: paying for "publishing" without verifying service quality.
Some so-called publishers are service sellers. They charge high fees for editing, cover design, and listing, but deliver weak work. The author pays, and the book still fails. If you pay for services, you must treat it like hiring professionals, not like buying a miracle.

Mistake six: losing control of pricing.
If you cannot control pricing, you cannot control your business model. Pricing affects margins, bulk sales, and positioning. A partner who underprices your book can harm your brand and make it hard to sustain production.

Mistake seven: losing access to files and production sources.
If a partner controls the formatted files, cover design files, and print-ready files, and you do not have them, you are trapped. Always keep your own copies and source files.

Mistake eight: confusing an endorsement with a contract.
Sometimes a person promises, "I will help you," and they ask you to sign something. Help can be given without owning your rights. If someone's help requires owning your work, that is not help. That is acquisition.

Mistake nine: trusting verbal promises.
If it is not written, it does not exist. Verbal promises disappear the moment there is conflict.

Mistake ten: partnering out of desperation.
Desperation makes you accept bad terms because you

want relief. Relief today can become slavery tomorrow. I would rather scale slowly than sign away my future.

Now, the checklist I use

This is the part I want you to keep as a tool. Every time I consider a publishing route, I run the decision through this checklist. It keeps me grounded.

First: What is the primary market for this book right now?
Is it local offline buyers?
Is it online global buyers?
Is it a specific organization or school network?
Is it a hybrid of both?

Second: What format will sell best for this market?
Paperback?
Ebook?
Both?
A workbook plus a main book?
Is an audio edition worth planning later?

Third: How fast do I need this book in the market?
If speed is critical, local printing might be faster.
If global reach matters more than speed, platforms might be better.
If a partner has distribution ready, partnership might be fastest.

Fourth: What is my cash position?
Can I fund printing myself?
Do I need print-on-demand to avoid inventory?
Do I need a sponsor for bulk printing?

Fifth: What level of control do I require?
Do I need full control of cover, pricing, and messaging?
Am I willing to share control for greater reach?
What is non-negotiable for me?

Sixth: What is the unit economics for each route?
What is the per-copy cost?
What is the expected margin at my price?
What is the break-even for one-time costs?

Seventh: What is the inventory risk?
If I print locally, how many copies can I realistically sell in a set period?
Where will I store them?
How will I move them?

Eighth: What is the distribution plan?
If offline, which channels will carry it?
If online, how will buyers find it?
What keywords, categories, and positioning will I use?
If partner, what distribution do they truly control?

Ninth: What rights am I giving up, if any?
Print rights, ebook rights, audio rights, translation rights, territory rights.
Are they exclusive?
For how long?
What compensation matches that loss of rights?

Tenth: What is the exit plan?
If the route fails, how do I recover?
Can I end the contract?
Can I move to another route?
Do I keep my files?
Do I have a clear termination clause?

Eleventh: What proof do I have that this route will work?
Has the printer produced quality books before?
Has the platform listing approach worked for similar books?
Has the partner successfully distributed books like mine?

Twelfth: What is the simplest route that matches my current reality?
Sometimes the best route is the one that requires the least complexity while still meeting the market. Complexity can wait. Consistency cannot.

Using the checklist in real scenarios

Now let me show you how this checklist looks in practice with examples.

Scenario one: A book aimed at schools in my region.
Primary market is offline.
Format is paperback.
Speed matters because the school term is running.
Cash position might allow a small print run.
Control is important because I need the book to match the curriculum tone.
Route: local printing, with a plan for bulk sales and school partnerships.

Scenario two: A niche nonfiction guide aimed at global online readers.
Primary market is online.
Format is ebook and print-on-demand paperback.
Speed matters but global reach matters more.
Cash position may be limited, so print-on-demand reduces inventory risk.

Route: self-publishing platform, plus a basic direct sales page later.

Scenario three: A sponsor wants to distribute my book through their network.
Primary market is the sponsor's distribution network.
Format is paperback in volume.
Cash is available from sponsor.
Control: I must protect my message and title and pricing.
Rights: I refuse to give copyright. I might grant print rights for a limited quantity or limited term.
Route: partnership with clear contract and performance conditions.

These examples show the point. The route depends on the book and the market, not on what other people are doing.

The tradeoffs I refuse to ignore

Let me state the tradeoffs plainly, because this is where my discipline shows.

I refuse to ignore control versus reach.
Reach can be bought with control. Sometimes that is worth it, sometimes it is not.

I refuse to ignore short-term cash versus long-term freedom.
A deal that gives me cash today but steals my rights for years is not a deal, it is a trap.

I refuse to ignore unit economics.
A route that looks prestigious but leaves me earning pennies is not sustainable.

I refuse to ignore performance requirements.
If someone holds my rights, they must be obligated to perform, and there must be consequences if they do not.

I refuse to ignore exit.
No route is perfect. I must be able to pivot if reality changes.

I refuse to ignore file ownership.
I keep my files. I keep my source documents. I keep my cover files. If I do not, I am not running a business. I am renting my own work.

Closing lesson

Let me close this chapter with a final teaching note.

Publishing routes are like roads through a forest. Some roads are smooth but long. Some are rough but short. Some are dangerous because they lead to places you cannot escape. A wise traveler does not choose a road because it looks exciting. A wise traveler chooses a road because it leads to a destination with minimum unnecessary risk.

So choose your route like a publisher.

Know your buyer.
Know your economics.
Know your rights.
Know your exit.

If you do that, you can use local printing, platforms, and partnerships with confidence. You will not be trapped.

You will not be rushed. You will build a book business that remains yours.

CHAPTER 10: SELF-PUBLISHING STEP BY STEP, WITHOUT CONFUSION

Self-publishing looks easy from the outside. Upload a file, add a cover, click publish, then wait for sales. That simple picture is why many good books get buried online. The process is not hard, but it is precise. One sloppy decision can reduce your discoverability, damage trust, or create technical problems that make readers quit and leave poor reviews. I learned to treat self-publishing like a production line. Each stage has a job. When every stage is done well, the listing goes live clean, the book reads well, and the market has no reason to doubt you.

I am going to walk you through the workflow from manuscript to live listing in a way that removes confusion. I will show you file prep basics, proofing, and launch timing. Then I will show you the rookie errors that bury books online, and how I avoid them. I will speak as the main guide because that is how I operate. I do not outsource my thinking. I may outsource tasks, but I keep control of the system.

Before I touch any platform, I lock the manuscript. This is the first discipline.

Locking the manuscript means I decide the book is done enough to become a product. Done enough does not mean perfect. It means the structure is solid, the promise is delivered, the language is clean, and the text is ready for final formatting. Many authors keep editing while formatting and uploading. That is how errors multiply. A stable manuscript creates a stable production process.

So I do one last full read as a reader, not as a writer. I check for missing steps, repeated sections, weak transitions, and places where the reader might get confused. I fix those. Then I freeze the text. Any changes after this point must be small and controlled.

Next, I decide the formats I am publishing first. I do not publish everything at once unless I have the capacity to do it well. The common formats are ebook and paperback, and sometimes hardcover later. Each format has its own file needs. If I try to do too much at once, I rush, and rushed publishing is expensive in hidden ways.

If the book is a practical guide like this one, I usually publish both ebook and paperback. The ebook is great for global reach and fast access. The paperback builds physical trust and works well for offline sales too. If I am targeting schools, events, and organizations, the paperback becomes critical.

Now I choose my publishing route and tool for the online listing. When people say "self-publishing," they often mean Amazon Kindle Direct Publishing, but it is not the only route. There is IngramSpark for wider bookstore and library distribution in many regions. There is Draft2Digital if I want to distribute ebooks to multiple stores without managing each one separately. There are also direct stores like Kobo and Apple Books, plus other options depending on where my readers buy. I do not get lost in the options. I pick based on the buyer and the plan for this book.

Once I choose where the book will go live, I prepare the core production assets. I treat these assets like the spine of the operation.

The core assets are the interior file, the cover file, the book description, and the metadata.

Let me start with the interior file, because the interior is where readers decide whether you are professional. A cover can attract a click, but the interior makes the reader stay.

For paperback, the interior file is usually a print-ready PDF. For ebooks, the interior is usually an EPUB file, sometimes created from a Word document and then converted properly. The big mistake is assuming that a Word document is already a book file. It is not. Word is a writing tool. A book file is a reading tool. They are not the same.

So I format the interior with the reader's eyes in mind. I choose a clean font that reads easily. I use consistent heading styles for chapter titles and section headers. I keep line spacing comfortable. I keep margins correct for the trim size. I avoid crowded pages because crowded pages feel cheap and tiring.

If the paperback will be printed, I set the trim size early and do not change it late. Trim size affects margins, page count, and cover spine width. If you change trim late, you create a chain reaction of rework.

I also handle front matter and back matter carefully. I keep the title page and copyright page as they are, just as you instructed. Then I make sure the table of contents, if used, matches the final chapter headings. If your chapter headings are "CHAPTER 10" style, that exact wording must match everywhere. Inconsistency signals carelessness.

For ebook formatting, I keep it simpler than print, because ebooks behave differently across devices. I avoid complex layouts that break on small screens. I avoid fancy spacing tricks. I rely on clean headings and clear paragraph styles. I test on a few screen sizes because what looks fine on a laptop can look messy on a phone.

Now, images and tables. If the book includes them, I treat them as potential failure points. Low-resolution images will look ugly and can cause rejection. Images placed poorly can shift and break layouts. If I do not truly need images in an ebook, I remove them or simplify them. If I do need them, I use proper resolution and placement rules for the platform.

Next, the cover file. The cover is not one picture. The paperback cover is a full wrap that includes front cover, spine, and back cover, plus bleed if required. This is where rookies get trapped. They design a front cover and forget the rest, or they guess the spine width, or they ignore bleed and safe zones.

So I always use the platform's cover template or calculator. The spine width depends on page count and paper type. Guessing produces misalignment. Misalignment looks amateur. Amateur packaging reduces conversions and makes you fight pricing.

I also make sure the title and subtitle are readable at thumbnail size. If the title is thin, small, or lost in the background, online browsing will punish the book. People scroll fast. Your cover must communicate in one second.

Then I prepare the book description. This is a business asset, not a literary essay. The description must do three jobs: make the promise clear, show who the book is for, and reduce doubt. I write it like a product page, but in a human voice.

I usually include a short opening that names the problem. Then I state the promise. Then I show what the reader will learn or be able to do. I also set expectations about the style, especially if the book uses story and teaching examples. Buyers should not wonder if it is a memoir, a textbook, or a devotional. I tell them what it is.

Now metadata. Metadata is what the online marketplace uses to decide where to place your book and which searches it appears in. Metadata includes title, subtitle, author name, series name and number if applicable, keywords, categories, book language, publication date, and sometimes age or audience settings.

I treat metadata like a map. If the map is wrong, the buyer never finds the book.

I keep the author name consistent across all books. If one book says "John Monyjok Maluth" and another says "J. M. Maluth" without a clear plan, you split your author identity and make it harder for readers to follow your catalog. Consistency matters more than style.

I choose categories that match buyer intent, not ego. Some authors choose categories that feel prestigious but have the wrong audience. Then they wonder why their book is invisible. If the book is a practical business guide, I do not place it in categories where readers expect literary essays. If the book is a writing craft guide, I do not bury it in general motivation. I match the shelf to the buyer.

Keywords are also about buyer intent. I choose phrases real buyers might type when they want the outcome the book provides. I do not stuff keywords inside the title like a desperate person. Many platforms penalize messy metadata. Also, keyword stuffing makes the book look cheap.

Once the assets are ready, I move to the platform setup and upload stage. This stage should feel boring. Boring is good. Boring means the system is under control.

I create the book listing draft. I enter title, subtitle, author name, description, keywords, and categories. I choose the publication territories and rights correctly. This is another trap. If you choose the wrong rights setting, you can block distribution or create legal trouble. I only claim rights I truly own.

Then I upload the interior file. The platform will usually run an automated previewer. I do not trust it blindly, but I use it as a first alarm system. I look for obvious errors: missing chapter breaks, strange spacing, broken headings, blank pages, weird symbols, or font problems.

Then I upload the cover. I check alignment. I check spine text. I check the back cover. I check barcode placement if the platform adds it. I check bleed and safe margins. If anything looks off, I fix it now, not after publication.

Now comes proofing, which is where professional self-publishers separate themselves from hopeful uploaders.

I proof in three layers.

First layer is digital preview proofing. I scroll every chapter in the previewer and look for layout issues. I do not skim this step. I scan it like a quality inspector.

Second layer is file proofing on real devices for ebooks. I view the EPUB on a phone and a tablet if possible. I check the table of contents, headings, paragraph spacing, and any links. A broken table of contents makes an ebook feel cheap immediately.

Third layer is physical proofing for print. I order a proof copy. I hold it. I flip it. I read parts of it. I check cover color, cover sharpness, spine alignment, paper feel, interior clarity, and binding quality. This is not vanity. This is product verification.

Many rookie errors that ruin reviews come from skipping physical proofing. A reader might forgive a small typo. They will not forgive pages falling out, gray printing, crooked covers, or cramped text. Those things produce one-star reviews that poison future sales.

Now let us talk about launch timing, because timing is not only a marketing issue. Timing affects production and error control.

I like to have a buffer period between final upload and public launch. That buffer gives me time to review proof copies, fix any issues, and prepare my marketing materials calmly. Rushing to publish on a specific date with no buffer is how authors lock in mistakes.

If I plan a preorder, I treat it as a commitment. A preorder is not a toy. It creates expectation. If I miss the date or upload a messy file, I disappoint buyers early, and disappointed buyers do not become promoters.

So I only set a preorder when the manuscript and production files are stable. If the book is still changing, I wait. It is better to launch later with strength than to launch early with embarrassment.

Now, how do I avoid rookie errors that bury books online? I will name the main ones and show how I prevent them, but I will do it in a way that keeps this chapter readable.

The first rookie error is weak packaging. The cover looks amateur, the title is unclear, and the subtitle does not state the promise. Online markets punish confusion. If the cover and title do not speak clearly, the book will not get clicks. Without clicks, the algorithm has nothing to work with. So I treat cover and title as the first marketing system.

The second rookie error is a bad description. Many authors write a description that sounds like a personal diary or a poem. They talk about themselves instead of the buyer. The buyer is asking, "What will this do for me?" If your description does not answer that, they leave. I write descriptions that lead with the reader's need, then the promise, then the content highlights, then the outcome.

The third rookie error is messy formatting. Ebooks with broken headings, random spacing, and inconsistent fonts feel unprofessional. Print books with tight margins and awkward spacing feel cheap. Readers quit. Quitting reduces completion. Low completion reduces referrals. So formatting is not cosmetic. It is conversion.

The fourth rookie error is publishing without proofing. I already said it, but it is worth repeating because this single mistake destroys many first books. If you cannot afford a proof copy, print a small local sample or use a cheaper approach, but do not publish blind. Blind publishing is a gamble with your brand name.

The fifth rookie error is wrong categories and weak keywords. If you put your book in the wrong shelf, the wrong buyers see it, and they do not buy. Or they buy and leave poor reviews because expectations were wrong. Correct categories and keywords bring the right buyers, and the right buyers produce better reviews and referrals.

The sixth rookie error is pricing without strategy. Some authors price too high without packaging to support it, so sales die. Others price too low, so they cannot afford ads, cannot reinvest, and cannot scale. I price based on buyer value, competitor expectations, and my own margin needs. I also remember that in many online stores, pricing affects perceived quality. A price that is too low can signal low value.

The seventh rookie error is publishing one book and stopping. Online selling rewards catalogs. A single book can sell, but a catalog multiplies visibility. Each book becomes a doorway to the others. This is why I do not publish and disappear. I publish, then I build the next asset.

The eighth rookie error is ignoring the author presence. Buyers often click your author name. If they find nothing, it reduces trust. So I build a simple author profile, even if it is basic. I make it easy for readers to see my other books. This is not ego. This is making the buying pathway smooth.

The ninth rookie error is inconsistent branding across a series. If the covers look like they belong to different authors, readers do not connect them. Consistent series design increases read-through. Read-through is when a buyer finishes one book and buys the next. That is the quiet engine of a book business.

The tenth rookie error is breaking platform rules. Some authors add misleading claims, fake reviews, or forbidden content in descriptions. That can get the listing removed or the account flagged. I refuse shortcuts that can destroy my catalog. Trust is slow to build and fast to lose.

Now let me walk you through my clean "from manuscript to live listing" sequence again, as a single flow, because confusion often comes from jumping around.

I finish the manuscript and lock it.

I format the interior for the chosen formats, keeping print and ebook needs separate.

I prepare the cover properly for paperback wrap, using correct spine measurements and bleed rules.

I write the description as a product promise, not as personal praise.

I choose metadata that matches buyer intent: categories, keywords, and consistent author identity.

I upload the files, review the previews, and fix issues.

I order a proof copy for print, and I test the ebook file on real devices.

I make final corrections and upload the final files.

I set a launch date only after the product is verified.

Then I go live.

When the book is live, I do not assume the work is finished. I check the listing as a buyer. I search for the book using a few likely buyer phrases. I see where it appears. I confirm the cover displays correctly. I confirm the description looks clean. I confirm the "look inside" feature, if available, does not show broken pages. These checks help me catch problems early.

Then I begin the post-launch discipline: driving traffic, collecting feedback, improving packaging if needed, and building the next title.

Let me add one final truth that made my self-publishing life simpler.

Self-publishing is not mainly a tech problem. It is a systems problem.

When you build a system, the tech becomes routine. When you chase hacks, the tech becomes chaos.

So I do not publish like a gambler. I publish like a producer.

I keep my files organized, with clear folder names and version control.

I keep a master document for metadata so I can reuse and stay consistent.
I keep a checklist for every release so I do not forget key steps.
I keep proofing as a non-negotiable step.
I keep launch timing calm, not rushed.

That is self-publishing step by step, without confusion. It is not magical. It is disciplined. And once you master it, you stop fearing the upload button. You start treating it like what it is: the final stage of turning your manuscript into a real product the world can find, trust, buy, and recommend.

CHAPTER 11: OFFLINE DISTRIBUTION THAT WORKS IN THE REAL WORLD

Online selling is powerful, but offline distribution is where many authors in our kind of markets either win or quit. Offline is where people still buy with their hands, where trust is built face to face, and where a book can move through communities faster than any algorithm. Offline is also where many authors fail, not because the market is impossible, but because they treat distribution like begging instead of building.

I learned early that printing books is not the same as distributing books. Printing is production. Distribution is placement. If a book stays in my house, it is not inventory, it is dead stock. The only way it becomes alive is when it is placed where buyers already gather, and when the buying process is simple.

This chapter is about offline distribution that works in the real world. I will teach how I place books in shops, schools, organizations, and events. I will show how I use bulk sales and partnerships instead of waiting for random customers. Then I will explain consignment, wholesale, receipts, and accountability, because without accountability, offline distribution becomes a leak.

The mindset shift: I am not "selling books," I am building channels

When I started, I thought selling meant standing somewhere and convincing strangers. That is exhausting. That is also unreliable. I now think like a distributor. A distributor builds channels where books can move without constant persuasion.

A channel is any place or system where the right buyer can encounter the book with low friction.

A bookshop is a channel.
A school is a channel.
A church bookstore table is a channel.
A training workshop is a channel.
An NGO office front desk is a channel.
A youth club meeting is a channel.
A conference registration desk is a channel.

Once you think this way, you stop chasing random customers and you start creating predictable access to buyers.

The core principle is simple.

I do not ask, "Where can I sell today?"
I ask, "Where do my buyers already gather every week?"

Then I place the book there.

Placing books in shops

Bookshops and stationery shops are obvious, but many authors approach them badly. They walk in with fear, they beg, they offer no clear terms, and they leave without an agreement. The shopkeeper forgets them the next day.

I approach shops like a business person.

I do not start with my life story.
I start with the product and the market fit.

I say, "This book is for this type of reader. People in this area ask for this topic. I want to place copies here so your customers can buy easily. Here are the terms."

Then I show the book. Packaging matters here. A book that looks professional is easier to place. A book that looks amateur forces the shopkeeper to take a risk with their shelf image.

Now, there are two common ways to place books in shops: wholesale and consignment.

Wholesale means the shop buys copies from me at a lower price and then resells at the retail price. The shop carries the risk of unsold copies, which is why they demand a discount.

Consignment means I place copies in the shop, the shop sells at the retail price, and then they pay me my share after sales. I carry the risk of unsold copies.

In many real markets, consignment is more common because shops do not want to spend cash upfront on unknown books. But consignment can destroy you if you do it without accountability.

So I decide based on the shop's trust level and my cash needs.

If the shop is reliable and has strong customer flow, consignment can be good.

If the shop is unreliable or has weak records, I push for wholesale or I avoid it.

If the shop insists on consignment, I set clear terms.

How many copies am I placing?
What is the retail price?
What is the shop's commission?
When will we reconcile sales and pay?
What happens to damaged or lost copies?
Who is responsible for theft?
What is the return policy?

If these are not clear, consignment becomes a donation.

I also start small. I might place five or ten copies first. Then I measure sales speed. If the shop sells, I add more. If the shop does not sell, I retrieve stock and try another channel.

This is how I avoid dead stock sitting in shops for months while I pretend I am "distributed."

Placing books in schools

Schools are one of the strongest offline channels because they have structured learning needs, repeated semesters, and bulk purchasing potential. But you cannot approach schools like a street market. Schools have authority structures.

The first question is, who decides?

Sometimes it is the head teacher.
Sometimes it is the academic director.

Sometimes it is the librarian.
Sometimes it is the department head.
Sometimes it is a school board.
Sometimes it is an owner if it is a private school.

So I do not waste time talking to someone who cannot decide. I respect people, but I respect time too. I politely ask who handles learning materials and purchasing. Then I speak to that person.

When I present a book to a school, I speak the school's language.

How does this book help students?
What outcomes does it improve?
How does it support the curriculum?
Can it be used for a club, a library, or a classroom program?
Is there a teacher guide or a simple reading plan inside?
Is the language appropriate?
Is it aligned to the students' level?

Schools care about results and reputation. If your book looks weak or the content feels unfocused, they will not risk it.

So I package the offer as a solution.

For example, if the book teaches study skills, I offer it as part of a student performance improvement plan. If it teaches writing, I offer it as a writing club resource with weekly exercises. If it is a life skills book, I offer it as a mentorship program tool.

Then I propose a bulk option.

Bulk sales are where the real money and impact often live in offline publishing. Selling one copy at a time is slow. Bulk orders move 50, 100, 200 copies at once. Bulk orders also reduce distribution effort because one sale event clears a lot of stock.

So I create bulk packages.

One package might be 30 copies for a reading club.
Another might be 100 copies for a grade level.
Another might be 200 copies for a whole school program.

I also offer a simple add-on: a workshop or talk.

A school may be more willing to buy if I also come to speak for one hour and guide students on how to use the book. This is not "free motivation." This is a value-added service that makes the purchase feel safer and more useful.

Placing books in organizations

Organizations include NGOs, churches, government offices, companies, and community groups. Many of them have training needs, staff development needs, or program content needs. Books can serve those needs, but only if you position them correctly.

The biggest mistake authors make is walking into an organization and saying, "Please buy my book."

Organizations do not buy books to support authors. They buy books to solve problems.

So I approach organizations like a consultant.

I ask what challenge they are trying to solve.
I identify whether my book supports that challenge.
I propose a bulk order and a simple implementation plan.

For example, an NGO running youth empowerment programs might need a practical guide to discipline and planning. A church running leadership training might need a discipleship or values-based leadership book. A company might need a training manual on communication or productivity.

If my book fits, I propose a partnership.

Partnerships in offline distribution are not always about rights. They are often about placement and repeated ordering.

An organization can become a repeat buyer if the book becomes part of their program.

This is how you stop waiting for random customers. You anchor sales into systems that already exist.

Placing books at events

Events are powerful because they gather your buyer type in one place. Events also create urgency. People are already spending on registration, transport, and food. Buying a book becomes part of the experience.

But events can also waste time if you attend without a plan.

I use two event strategies.

Strategy one is table sales.
I get permission to set up a small table. I display books cleanly. I keep pricing clear. I have change or a payment method ready. I keep the pitch short. I do not pressure. I let the book and the promise do the work.

Strategy two is bulk placement through the organizer.
This is stronger.

If the event has 100 attendees, I can propose that the organizer includes my book as part of the event package. They buy 100 copies at a bulk rate. Every attendee receives the book. Now my book reaches 100 target readers instantly. Some will later buy my other books. Some will invite me to speak elsewhere. Some will recommend.

This is how events become growth engines, not just small sales days.

Bulk sales and partnerships instead of random customers

Let me speak directly about the difference between random sales and bulk sales.

Random sales are unpredictable.
Bulk sales are planned.

Random sales depend on mood, luck, and daily hustle. Bulk sales depend on relationships, proposals, and clear terms.

If I want a stable book business, I cannot rely only on random sales.

So I build bulk pathways on purpose.

I make a list of potential bulk buyers:

Schools.
Churches and church networks.
NGOs running trainings.
Youth clubs.
Universities.
Government training departments.
Companies with staff development programs.
Bookstores and stationery chains.
Event organizers.

Then I approach them with an offer that reduces risk.

I show the value.
I offer a bulk rate.
I offer a simple implementation plan.
I provide clear documentation and receipts.
I propose delivery and follow-up.

This turns the conversation from "buy my book" into "here is a solution you can deploy."

Now we come to the technical side: consignment, wholesale, receipts, and accountability.

Many authors hate this part. They want to stay in the creative zone. But if you avoid accountability, you will lose stock and money. You will also damage relationships because partners will not trust you if you are disorganized.

So I treat accountability as a form of integrity.

Consignment explained clearly

Consignment means I place copies at a shop or partner location without being paid upfront. The partner sells the books and then pays me after sales.

The risk for me is that books can disappear, the partner can delay payment, or the partner can lie about sales.

So I protect myself with simple rules.

I always use a consignment agreement, even if it is one page.
It includes:
The date.
The partner name and location.
The book title.
The number of copies placed.
The retail price.
The commission percentage or amount.
The payment schedule.
The responsibility for damage or loss.
The signature of both parties.

I keep a copy. They keep a copy.

Then I label the consigned books or record their batch number so I can track.

I also set a clear reconciliation date.
For example, every two weeks or every month, we count stock and sales.

If a partner refuses clear reconciliation, I do not consign. I would rather sell directly than lose slowly.

Wholesale explained clearly

Wholesale means the partner buys copies from me at a discounted price, and they sell at the retail price.

The risk for me is lower because I get paid upfront. The risk for the partner is higher because they carry stock risk.

Wholesale is cleaner for cash flow.

But I must set the wholesale price carefully. It must still leave me profit after per-copy costs.

In Chapter 8, I showed how margin changes with wholesale pricing. That math must guide wholesale decisions. If the wholesale price leaves me almost nothing, I am not building a business. I am building stress.

Receipts and accountability

Receipts are not only for big companies. Receipts are for anyone who wants to be trusted.

When I sell to a bulk buyer or place books in consignment, I issue a receipt.

A receipt includes:
Date.
Buyer name and contact.
Quantity.
Unit price.
Total amount.
Payment status: paid, part-paid, or owed.
Signature.

If it is consignment, I still issue a placement receipt, showing quantity placed and terms.

Why does this matter?

Because memory lies.
Because people change.
Because staff turnover happens.
Because misunderstandings happen.
Because trust is built with records.

When you keep receipts and records, disputes become rare. When disputes arise, you resolve them calmly with facts.

This is what I mean by accountability.

Accountability also includes stock tracking.

If I place ten copies in a shop, and after a month five are sold, I record it.
If I collect payment for five, I record it.
If I replace stock, I record it.

This record keeps my business real. Without records, the business becomes a story I tell myself.

How I manage payment and reduce debt

In offline markets, many buyers will want to take books and "pay later." That can work, but it can also destroy you.

So I create payment rules.

For new partners, I prefer full payment upfront.
If they cannot pay upfront, I require a deposit.
If they have a strong reputation and relationship, I can allow delayed payment with clear terms and dates.

I do not allow vague promises like "I will pay you when I sell." That is consignment, and consignment has rules. If they want consignment, we do consignment properly. If they want credit, we do credit properly with dates.

If you allow vague promises, you will become a bank, and you will suffer.

Now, I want to address a reality. Offline distribution often operates inside relationship culture. People may feel offended when you demand receipts and clear terms. They may say you do not trust them. I handle that with calm honesty.

I say, "This is how I run the book work so everything stays clear and respectful. It protects both of us. It prevents misunderstanding."

When you say it like that, serious people respect you more. And unserious people reveal themselves early, which saves you.

Building a distribution rhythm

Offline distribution is not a one-time push. It is a rhythm.

I build a weekly rhythm.

One day is for visiting channels and checking stock.
One day is for meetings with bulk buyers or proposals.
One day is for deliveries and payment collection.
One day is for events or community gatherings.
One day is for planning and records.

This rhythm turns offline distribution into a predictable system.

If you only distribute when you are desperate, you will look desperate, and people will treat you casually. If you distribute consistently, you look like a real publisher, and people take you seriously.

A final teaching example

Let me use a simple example to bring everything together.

Nyakor runs a school reading club. She wants 30 copies of my book for students. If I treat this like random sales, I might sell her two copies today and hope she comes back later. That is slow and uncertain.

Instead, I treat it as bulk distribution.

I meet her. I present the program idea.
I offer 30 copies at a bulk price.
I provide a simple reading plan for four weeks.
I issue a receipt.
I deliver the books.
I follow up after two weeks to see how students respond.
If it works, Nyakor tells another school. That becomes another bulk order.

This is how books spread in real communities. Not by shouting, but by placing.

Closing lesson

Offline distribution is not inferior to online. It is different. It is human. It is relationship-based. It is built on trust, structure, and clear agreements.

If you want offline distribution that works, remember this.

Place books where buyers already gather.
Use bulk sales to create predictable volume.
Use partnerships to turn one-time buyers into repeat channels.
Treat consignment with discipline, not hope.
Treat wholesale with clean math.
Use receipts and records to protect integrity.
Build a weekly distribution rhythm so the work stays steady.

When you do this, your books stop waiting in boxes. They start living in the real world, moving through schools, shops, offices, and gatherings, carried by trust rather than pressure.

CHAPTER 12: ONLINE DISTRIBUTION AND DISCOVERABILITY

Online distribution is not magic. It is a system of shelves, search boxes, and buyer habits. The buyer is not wandering in a street market where they see your face and decide to support you. Online, the buyer is moving fast. They are searching, scanning, comparing, and deciding in seconds. If my book does not show up when the buyer searches, it is invisible. If it shows up but looks unclear, it gets skipped. If it gets clicked but does not match the buyer's intent, it gets abandoned, and the store learns that my book is not a good match.

So I treat online discoverability like a job I can learn. Not a lottery. Not a prayer. A job.

There are three truths I keep in my mind every time I publish online.

The first truth is that online stores do not "promote books." They match buyers to books. If I want my book to be matched, I must help the store understand who the buyer is and what my book delivers.

The second truth is that online buyers do not buy a book because it exists. They buy because they believe it solves a problem, satisfies a desire, or completes a plan they already have in their mind.

The third truth is that I do not control the algorithm, but I do control the signals I send: the cover, the title, the subtitle, the description, the categories, the keywords, the price, the sample pages, and the way I drive traffic from outside the store.

That is why this chapter is practical. I will explain how buyers find books online, and how I make my book show up. I will explain keywords, categories, descriptions, and the buyer-intent approach. Then I will show how I use direct sales as a serious long-term channel, because depending only on marketplaces is like building a house on rented land.

How online buyers find books

Online buyers usually find books in five ways.

They search for a problem they want to solve.

They browse categories and subcategories the way they browse aisles.

They click "also bought" and related recommendations after buying something similar.

They respond to outside traffic: social posts, email, blog articles, podcasts, or someone sharing a link.

They follow an author they already trust.

If I understand those five paths, I stop guessing. I start building signals for each path.

Search is the most obvious, so let me begin there. When a buyer searches, they are typing their need into the store. They are not typing my book title, because they do not know it yet. They are typing a phrase that sounds like their pain, their desire, or their plan.

If a buyer wants to earn money with books, they type things like "self publishing guide," "how to sell books," "book marketing," "publish on kindle," "sell books offline," "write and publish," or more specific phrases like "how to price a paperback" or "book keywords."

Notice what is happening. The buyer is not thinking about me. They are thinking about themselves. That is the heart of discoverability. My job is to connect the buyer's words to my book's promise.

Browsing is the second path. Some buyers do not search with clear phrases. They browse a category such as business, writing, publishing, marketing, entrepreneurship, or self-help, then narrow down. These buyers are still intent-driven, but their intent is less precise. They want "something in this area." My category choices matter for these buyers.

Recommendations are the third path. Stores recommend books based on buyer behavior. If people who bought Book A often buy Book B, the store starts showing Book B near Book A. This is why similar positioning matters. If my metadata points my book to the wrong neighborhood, I lose the chance of being recommended next to the right books.

Outside traffic is the fourth path. This is where I bring the buyer to the store instead of waiting for the store to bring the buyer to me. Outside traffic can wake up a listing that is quiet. It can also teach the store what kind of buyer likes my book. If the outside traffic converts, the store gains confidence in the book.

Author-following is the fifth path. This path grows over time. A catalog grows it faster, because each book becomes a doorway to the others. When someone likes one book, they want more. That is why I do not publish one book and stop. I build a trail.

Now I will show you the buyer-intent approach, because without it, keywords and categories become random.

Buyer intent is simply this: what the buyer is trying to do right now.

Some buyers have learning intent. They want to understand.

Some buyers have action intent. They want steps.

Some buyers have shopping intent. They want the best option.

Some buyers have comparison intent. They want to decide between choices.

Some buyers have urgency intent. They want a quick solution.

A buyer typing "what is self publishing" is at a different stage from a buyer typing "self publishing checklist" or "best self publishing book." Both are buyers, but their words reveal their stage. If my book is a step-by-step guide, I must meet action intent strongly. If my book is more reflective, I meet learning intent strongly.

This approach keeps me honest. It stops me from trying to appeal to everyone. It also shapes my description and my keywords. I do not only ask, "What is my topic?" I ask, "What is the buyer trying to do?"

Keywords that match real intent

Keywords are not a place for creativity. They are a place for accuracy. The goal is not to impress the store. The goal is to match the language a buyer uses.

I build keywords in three layers.

The first layer is the main problem phrase. This is the core search term people use. For this book, it might be "sell books," "book business," "self publishing," "book marketing," "publishing business," "author business," or "how to publish."

The second layer is the outcome phrase. This is what the buyer wants to achieve. Phrases like "make money with books," "sell more books," "earn from writing," "build a catalog," "grow book sales," "publish and sell," "book income," or "book launch plan" can sit here.

The third layer is the method phrase. This is how the buyer wants to do it. Phrases like "step by step," "checklist," "without ads," "offline and online," "pricing and royalties," "keywords and categories," "distribution plan," and "direct sales" can sit here.

When I combine these layers, I stop using vague keywords and I start using buyer language.

I also avoid a common trap: stuffing keywords that do not belong. If my book is not mainly about children's books, I do not chase children's book keywords just because they have traffic. Wrong traffic is worse than no traffic. Wrong traffic clicks and leaves. That trains the store to distrust the listing.

I also avoid repeating the same word in ten ways when the platform already understands it. Keyword slots are limited. I prefer variety that still matches intent.

Here is how I test a keyword idea without acting like a gambler.

I ask: if someone typed this phrase, would they be happy to land on my book?

If the answer is no, I remove the phrase. This one question protects my listing from confusion.

Categories that place me on the right shelf

Categories are the online version of physical shelving. They decide where the book appears when people browse, and they also influence which books the store recommends near yours.

A category is not a trophy. It is a neighborhood.

If my book is a practical guide for selling books, it must live near practical publishing and marketing books, not near unrelated motivation books just because the motivation category is easier. I would rather compete in the right neighborhood than win attention in the wrong one.

When I choose categories, I consider three things.

The first is relevance. The category must match what the buyer expects from the title, cover, and description.

The second is competition. Some categories are crowded with giants. Crowded is not automatically bad, but it changes what I need to succeed. In a crowded category, my cover, promise, and reviews must be stronger to stand out. In a less crowded but still relevant category, my book can surface faster.

The third is buyer behavior. Some categories attract buyers who actually purchase, not just browse. A category can have traffic but poor buying behavior. I pay attention to where buyers in my niche usually buy.

I also refuse to play category tricks that create disappointment. If I place my book in a category where readers expect a different kind of book, I might get a few accidental sales, but I will get poor reactions. Poor reactions can show up as refunds, low ratings, or weak engagement. That hurts long-term.

Descriptions that convert clicks into purchases

A cover wins the click. The description wins the purchase.

Many authors write descriptions like they are writing a personal statement. They talk about their childhood, their passion, or their mission. There is a place for mission, but the description is not mainly about me. It is about what the buyer gets.

I write descriptions with a simple discipline.

I name the problem in the buyer's words.

I state the promise clearly.

I show what is inside in a way that feels organized, not crowded.

I tell the buyer who the book is for.

I tell the buyer what changes when they apply it.

Then I invite them to buy.

I also match the tone of the book. If the book teaches with first-person stories and examples, the description should signal that. If the book is a strict manual, the description should signal that. A mismatch creates disappointment.

I also use clarity as a trust signal. Clear descriptions reduce refunds and reduce regret. When buyers know what they are getting, they buy with confidence.

One more thing about descriptions: I treat the first lines as precious. Online buyers often see only the first lines before they click "read more." Those first lines must carry the promise. If I waste them on vague poetry, the buyer scrolls away.

The sample pages are part of selling

Online stores often provide a sample, sometimes called "look inside" or a preview. This sample is not decoration. It is part of conversion.

If the first pages of my book are messy, cramped, or confusing, the buyer leaves. If the table of contents looks strong and clean, the buyer feels guided. If the opening pages show clear chapter structure and easy reading, the buyer feels safe.

So I treat formatting as marketing too. I do not hide behind "content matters more." Content matters, but presentation is how content enters the mind.

Pricing is also a discoverability signal

Price affects conversion, but it also affects how the store treats the book. If my price is too high for the category without strong packaging and trust signals, conversion drops. If conversion drops, the store shows the book less.

If my price is too low, buyers may assume low quality, and my margin may be too thin to sustain promotion. I price with sustainability and category expectation in mind.

I also think in terms of entry and ladder.

Sometimes an ebook can be priced as an easier entry for new buyers. The paperback can carry higher value because it is physical. Over time, a catalog creates a ladder where one book leads to another. The goal is not to squeeze the buyer. The goal is to build a long relationship.

Distribution options and what they really mean

When I self-publish, I choose how wide or how focused my distribution will be.

If I publish only through Amazon Kindle Direct Publishing, I can reach a massive marketplace and use its tools, but I must accept that I am building inside one ecosystem. That can be good, but I must manage the risk of dependence.

If I want broader print reach, I may use IngramSpark for access to many stores and libraries in places where that matters. This route can add complexity and cost, but it can also open doors.

If I want wide ebook distribution without managing each store, I can use Draft2Digital to reach multiple retailers through one dashboard. That can be a clean way to go wide, especially when time is limited.

If my readers are strong on specific retailers, I pay attention. Some niches do well on Kobo, some do well on Apple Books, and some do well on Google Play Books. The point is not to chase every store. The point is to match the buyer's habits.

I do not pick distribution based on noise. I pick it based on buyer location, payment habits, reading devices, and my ability to manage the workflow.

How I make my book show up, step by step

I start with the promise statement. I do not touch keywords before I can say the promise in one clear sentence. If the promise is foggy, the metadata will be foggy, and the listing will drift.

Then I craft the title and subtitle to carry that promise. I do not rely on the description to rescue an unclear title. The title and subtitle are the strongest signals.

Then I choose categories that match the promise and the buyer's shelf expectations.

Then I choose keywords that match how buyers speak when they are trying to solve that problem.

Then I write a description that matches those keywords and categories, and that makes the buyer feel guided.

Then I make sure the cover looks like it belongs in that category. Online buyers are trained by patterns. If my cover looks like a novel but my book is a business guide, the store gets confused and the buyer gets confused. Confused people do not buy.

Then I make sure the sample pages support the promise with clean formatting and visible structure.

Then I drive outside traffic that matches the same intent. This is important. If I drive random traffic, it will click and leave. If I drive the right traffic, it will convert, and conversion teaches the store to show the book more.

This is why I do not only promote "my book." I promote the buyer's problem and solution.

Instead of shouting "buy my book," I teach a small piece of the solution in a post, then I offer the book as the full system. That is how serious online selling works.

Direct sales as a serious long-term channel

Now I will talk about direct sales, because this is where many authors stay small by choice without realizing it.

Marketplace sales are good, but they come with limits.

The marketplace controls the shelf.

The marketplace controls the buyer relationship.

The marketplace can change rules, change visibility, and change fees.

If I want stability, I build a channel I control.

Direct sales means selling the book from my own site or store, collecting payment directly, and delivering the product directly.

Some authors treat direct sales like a side hobby. I treat it as a serious long-term channel, because it creates three forms of freedom.

It gives me higher margins.

It gives me direct access to the buyer, which means I can follow up, support, and offer the next book.

It reduces platform dependence.

Direct sales also fits my offline life. If I am already selling paperbacks in events and schools, direct sales becomes the online version of the same thing: I control the stock and the customer relationship.

But direct sales must be built with discipline. If the buying experience is messy, people will not trust it.

So I build direct sales like a small shop with clear rules.

The buyer must see a clear promise.

The buyer must be able to pay easily.

The buyer must receive the product reliably.

The buyer must know how to contact me if something goes wrong.

If I sell ebooks directly, I must deliver the file quickly and safely.

If I sell print books directly, I must manage shipping and packaging with care.

If I sell bundles, I must make the bundle benefits obvious.

Direct sales also allows me to do something marketplaces do not do well: create pathways.

A pathway is how I guide a reader from one book to the next.

On a marketplace, the store decides what else to show. On my own site, I decide. I can say, "If you bought this book, the next step is this other book." I can bundle them. I can offer a reader discount. I can offer a workbook add-on. I can offer a short course. I can build a catalog that feels like a guided journey rather than a pile of separate products.

This is how I stop relying on a single title.

Direct sales also works well with email.

When a buyer buys directly, I can invite them to join my list, receive updates, and get support. This is not spam. It is service. A reader who benefits from one book often wants the next. Email is how I keep that relationship alive without begging.

Let me use a simple teaching example.

Mama Ajok buys my book at an event. She likes it, but later she cannot find my next book easily online. If I have a direct sales page with clear links and a simple buying process, I can tell her, "If you want the next book, here is where to get it." Now she is not wandering. She is guided.

Mr. Aldridge buys a leadership book for his team. If I can offer him direct bulk ordering with an invoice and delivery plan, he becomes a repeat buyer. Marketplaces are not built for that kind of relationship. Direct sales is.

Nyakor buys a writing guide for her students. If I can offer a direct bundle for her class with a teacher plan included, she can deploy it faster. That is direct sales serving real needs.

How I combine marketplace and direct sales without confusion

I do not treat this as "either or." I treat it as "both, with roles."

Marketplaces are great for discovery, especially for buyers who already shop there.

Direct sales is great for relationship, margin, and stability.

So I let marketplaces do what they do best: help strangers find me.

And I let direct sales do what it does best: turn those strangers into long-term readers.

I also keep my messaging aligned. The promise is the same. The buyer language is the same. The pathway is clear.

A final discipline that protects discoverability

Online discoverability is not something I set once and forget. It is something I maintain.

I watch what people respond to.

If a title confuses buyers, I sharpen the subtitle.

If a cover does not get clicks, I improve it.

If the description is not converting, I rewrite the opening lines.

If keywords bring the wrong buyers, I change them.

If a category is wrong, I move.

I do not panic. I adjust. This is publishing as business, not publishing as emotion.

And I keep building the catalog, because one book can open a door, but a catalog builds a house.

So my rule in online distribution is simple.

Help the right buyer find the book.
Help the buyer trust the promise.
Help the buyer enjoy the reading experience.
Help the buyer take the next step.

When I do that consistently, the store starts showing the book more, readers start recommending it more, and my business starts depending less on loud promotion and more on quiet, steady discoverability.

CHAPTER 13: MARKETING THAT DOES NOT DRAIN MY LIFE

I used to think marketing meant noise. Post every day. Beg for attention. Show my book everywhere. Push harder when sales drop. That kind of marketing can work for a short burst, but it burns the author. It also cheapens the book, because people start to feel you are selling to survive, not selling because you have something worth buying.

I chose a different path because I want a book business that lasts. I want my writing life to be livable. I want to publish many books, not just one. That means my marketing must be sustainable.

So I built marketing that does not drain my life. Marketing that fits inside a normal week. Marketing that can be repeated for years. Marketing that can still work when my internet is weak, my power is unstable, and my schedule is busy. Marketing that is more like planting than begging.

In this chapter, I will teach my weekly promotion routine that stays sustainable. I will show how I repurpose one idea into many posts without sounding repetitive. Then I will explain how I use email and simple follow-up to create repeat buyers, because repeat buyers are the quiet engine of a calm publishing business.

The mindset that makes marketing sustainable

Sustainable marketing begins with a mindset change.

I do not market books. I market outcomes.

People do not wake up and say, "I want to support Panyim by buying his book." They wake up and say, "I want to solve this problem," or "I want to improve my life," or "I want to learn something," or "I want to feel inspired in a real way." The book is the tool they buy to reach that outcome.

So when I market, I lead with the problem and the promise, not the product.

That makes marketing easier because I always have something useful to say. I am not repeating "buy my book." I am teaching, guiding, and sharing a small piece of the solution. Then I invite the reader to get the full system inside the book.

The second mindset change is this.

I do not chase attention. I build trust.

Attention can be cheap. Trust is expensive. Trust is built by consistency, clarity, and service.

If I publish consistently, if I speak clearly, if I help people, they begin to trust me. When trust grows, marketing becomes lighter. I do not need to push as hard because people listen with less resistance.

The third mindset change is this.

Marketing is a routine, not an emergency.

When marketing becomes an emergency, you panic. You post randomly. You sound desperate. You try shortcuts. You burn out.

When marketing is a routine, you do small actions regularly. Small actions compound. That is how you stay alive in this business.

My weekly promotion routine that stays sustainable

Now I will show you the weekly routine I use. It is simple on purpose. Complexity looks impressive, but it often collapses under real life.

I structure my week around four actions:

One content anchor.
Three small distribution touches.
One relationship follow-up block.
One review and adjustment session.

Let me explain each one.

One content anchor is the main piece of content I create for the week. This is the thing that carries real value. It can be a blog post, a long social post, a short article, a teaching thread, a video script, a podcast note, or even a live talk summary. The format can change, but the principle stays the same: one anchor that teaches something clear.

I choose the anchor based on one question.

What is one problem my buyer is struggling with right now?

If my book is about books as a business, the problems might be:

How to price a paperback.
How to choose keywords.
How to sell offline.
How to stop procrastinating and finish.
How to build a catalog.
How to approach schools and organizations.
How to avoid bad publishing deals.
How to build direct sales.

Each week I pick one. Just one. This keeps me focused.

Then I create three small distribution touches. Distribution touches are small ways I spread the anchor content across places where my buyers already are.

For example:

I post a short version of the idea on one social platform.
I post a different angle of the same idea on another platform.
I share a short story example related to the idea in a group or community.

These are not separate topics. They are the same topic in different clothes.

Then I do one relationship follow-up block. This is where many authors fail. They post content, but they do not follow up with human connection. They treat marketing like broadcasting. But books move through relationships.

So each week, I set aside one block of time to do follow-up.

I reply to comments and questions.
I message key contacts who might become partners.
I check in with a school leader or an organization I spoke with.
I thank readers who shared the book.
I ask one buyer how the book helped them.

This follow-up is not spam. It is service. It turns readers into friends and friends into promoters.

Then I do one review and adjustment session at the end of the week.

I look at what happened.
What content got responses?
What questions did people ask?
What link got clicks?
What channel felt alive?
What channel felt dead?
What did I enjoy doing?
What drained me?

Then I adjust the next week. I do not overthink. I make small improvements.

This is the weekly routine. One anchor, three touches, one follow-up block, one review.

It does not drain me because it fits inside real life. It does not require me to be online all day. It does not require me to be famous. It requires me to be consistent.

Now let me show you how I execute it in a practical way.

Monday or Tuesday, I create the anchor.
Wednesday, I extract the first small post.
Thursday, I extract the second small post.
Friday, I extract the third small post or a story clip.
Saturday, I do follow-up.
Sunday, I review and plan.

Sometimes the days change, but the rhythm remains.

If I miss a week, I do not quit. I restart. The point is consistency over perfection.

How I repurpose one idea into many posts without sounding repetitive

Many people say "repurpose content," but they do it in a lazy way. They copy and paste the same message everywhere. That becomes repetitive, and people mute you.

Repurposing properly is not copying. It is translating.

I translate one idea into different forms that fit different attention spans and different situations.

I use a simple repurposing map.

One idea can be expressed as:

A lesson.
A story.
A checklist.
A myth versus truth.
A mistake to avoid.
A quick tip.

A question and answer.
A short case study.
A personal reflection.

All of these can come from the same idea.

Let me demonstrate with one idea, so you see the method.

Suppose the anchor idea is: "Your book needs a clear promise statement."

The long anchor might be a full post explaining how to write a promise statement and how it connects to the cover and description.

Now the repurposing looks like this.

Lesson post:
"Here is how I write a promise statement in one sentence."

Story post:
"I once published a book with no clear promise, and it sat in boxes."

Checklist post:
"Three questions your promise must answer."

Myth versus truth:
"Myth: a good title is enough. Truth: the subtitle must clarify the promise."

Mistake to avoid:
"Do not write for applause. Write for outcomes."

Quick tip:
"If you cannot explain the book in one breath, the buyer cannot buy fast."

Question post:
"What is the one outcome your reader should get after finishing your book?"

Case study:
"I changed a subtitle and sales increased because buyers finally understood the offer."

Reflection:
"When I started thinking like a publisher, clarity became my discipline."

See what happened. Same idea, different angles. That is not repetition. That is reinforcement.

Reinforcement is good because buyers need to hear a truth more than once before they act. People are busy. They forget. Repetition becomes annoying only when it is word-for-word and empty. When it is varied and useful, it builds trust.

So I repurpose by changing the angle, not by changing the truth.

I also repurpose by changing the length.

A long post becomes a short post.
A short post becomes a quote card or a simple image caption.
A quote becomes a question.
A question becomes a reply thread.

A reply thread becomes a small FAQ.
A FAQ becomes a section in a future book.

This is how a catalog of content is built without draining.

I keep a simple "idea bank" for this.

Whenever someone asks a question about publishing, marketing, printing, or selling, I record it. That question becomes future content. This means I do not sit down and stare at a blank screen begging for ideas. The audience gives me ideas through their needs.

How I use email and simple follow-up to create repeat buyers

Now let us talk about repeat buyers, because repeat buyers are the difference between a stressful business and a calm business.

If I only make one-time sales, I must constantly find new buyers. That is exhausting.

If I create repeat buyers, my marketing becomes lighter because my existing readers keep buying the next book.

Email is one of the simplest ways to build repeat buyers, but many authors misuse email. They either ignore it or abuse it.

I treat email like a relationship channel, not a sales cannon.

The purpose of email is:

To stay in touch with readers who already trust me.
To deliver ongoing value so trust grows.
To guide readers to the next useful step when they are ready.

The first step is collecting emails in a respectful way.

I give readers a reason to join.

It might be a free chapter.
It might be a checklist.
It might be a reading plan.
It might be a short "publisher's toolkit" PDF.
It might be updates on new releases.
It might be a weekly teaching note.

The key is that it must be useful. People do not give emails for nothing anymore. They give emails for value.

In the book itself, I also include a clear invitation.

"If this book helped you, join my list to get the next lesson and the next release."

That simple line turns a book into a relationship gateway.

Now, what do I send?

I keep it simple: one email per week or one email every two weeks. The frequency depends on my capacity, but consistency matters more than frequency.

Each email has three parts.

A short story or lesson.
A practical takeaway.
A next step.

The next step might be:
"Reply and tell me what you are working on."
Or it might be:
"Here is the next book if you want deeper help."
Or it might be:
"Here is a free checklist to support your work."

Notice the tone. It is service, not pressure.

Follow-up is also part of email marketing.

If someone buys directly, I send a thank-you email and a simple guide on how to use the book. Then a few days later, I send a follow-up: "How is it going? What chapter helped you most?" This makes the reader feel seen. It also gives me feedback that improves future content and future books.

If someone attends a workshop and buys, I follow up with a resource and an invitation to join the list.

These small follow-ups create repeat buyers because they turn transactions into relationships.

The simplest repeat-buyer pathway

Now I want to give you a very simple repeat-buyer pathway you can use even if your systems are basic.

Book 1 is the entry book. It solves one clear problem.

Book 2 is the next step. It builds on Book 1.

Book 3 deepens or specializes further.

Inside Book 1, I mention Book 2 clearly.
Inside Book 2, I mention Book 3 clearly.

On my email list, I highlight the next step naturally.

If a reader loved the offline distribution chapter, I suggest the book that goes deeper on sales systems. If a reader loved the writing discipline chapter, I suggest the book that goes deeper on finishing and publishing routines.

This is not pushing. It is guiding.

When you guide readers properly, they buy more willingly because they feel you are helping them, not draining them.

Marketing boundaries that protect my life

Now let me speak about boundaries, because the chapter title is not a slogan. Marketing can drain you if you do not set rules.

I use these boundaries.

I do not post all day.
I choose a time window for marketing.
Outside that window, I write, publish, or live.

I do not argue online.
Arguments drain energy and rarely sell books.
If someone attacks, I respond briefly or not at all.

I do not chase every platform.
I pick two or three places where my buyers actually are.
I show up there consistently.
Everything else is optional.

I do not measure success by likes.
I measure by meaningful signs: replies, questions, email sign-ups, direct messages, bulk leads, sales.

I do not promote every day.
I teach more than I sell.
Selling is easier when teaching builds trust.

I also keep a "minimum marketing" plan for hard weeks.

Some weeks life hits hard. Power fails. Internet fails. Family problems rise. In those weeks, I do the minimum:

One short post.
One email.
Five replies to comments or messages.

That is enough to keep the engine warm. Consistency matters.

A practical example of a sustainable marketing week

Let me show you what a real week could look like for this book.

Anchor content:
A blog post titled "How I Sell Books Offline Without Begging."

Touch 1:
A short social post listing three places to place books: schools, churches, organizations.

Touch 2:
A story post about the first time I tried consignment and learned the need for receipts.

Touch 3:
A question post: "Where do your buyers gather every week?"

Follow-up block:
Reply to comments and messages.
Send two proposals to schools or organizations.

Email:
A teaching note summarizing the anchor with a small checklist, plus a link to the book.

Review:
Look at what people responded to and plan next week's topic.

That is marketing without exhaustion. It is steady. It is useful. It is repeatable.

Closing lesson

Marketing that does not drain your life is built on three pillars.

A routine you can keep.
Repurposing that feels like service, not noise.
Follow-up that turns buyers into repeat readers.

If you build these pillars, you will stop treating marketing as a burden and start treating it as part of the publishing craft. You will publish, you will share, you will connect, and you will keep your peace.

That is the goal. Not loud success for one week, but a calm, growing book business that stays alive year after year.

CHAPTER 14: LAUNCH WEEK, THEN THE REAL WORK AFTER LAUNCH WEEK

Launch week is important, but launch week is not the business. Launch week is the opening ceremony. The business is what happens when the crowd goes home and the chairs are stacked again. Many authors pour all their energy into seven days, then collapse. They call it "a great launch," but three weeks later the book is quiet, the author is tired, and the next book is not moving forward.

I learned to treat launch week as a disciplined sprint inside a longer race. The goal of launch week is not to feel celebrated. The goal is to create momentum that can be maintained with a calm routine after the excitement fades.

In this chapter, I will teach a clean launch plan for offline and online. I will show what I track daily during launch and what I ignore. Then I will explain how I keep selling after the excitement fades, because that is where real publishers separate themselves from one-time sprinters.

The clean launch plan

A clean launch plan begins before launch week. If I wait until launch week to prepare, I will rush, and rushed launches produce messy results. So I plan in three phases.

Pre-launch preparation
Launch week execution
Post-launch continuation

Pre-launch preparation is where I build the assets and remove friction.

For offline, I make sure I have stock. I do not want to "launch" with five copies. I decide the first print run based on the channels I will activate. If I have a school partnership that can move 100 copies, I must have at least that amount ready or a confirmed delivery date.

I also prepare basic materials: a simple one-page flyer or a clean image that explains what the book is, who it is for, and what problem it solves. I prepare a short talk outline in case I have to introduce the book in front of people. I set a clear price and a clear bulk offer. I print receipts or prepare an invoice template. I set up a simple way to receive payments and to track what is owed.

For online, I make sure the listing is strong before I ask people to click. I confirm the cover displays correctly, the description reads clean, the keywords and categories match the promise, and the sample pages look professional. If I sell directly, I make sure the checkout works and delivery is reliable. A broken link in launch week is like opening a shop with the door locked.

I also prepare the launch message itself. I do not write ten different messages. I write one core message and translate it for different channels. The core message has three parts: the problem, the promise, and the call to action.

Now we move into launch week execution.

Launch week execution for offline and online can be simple if you focus on a few high-impact actions instead of trying everything.

Offline launch week

My offline launch week has three pillars: a main launch gathering, bulk activation, and daily placement.

The main launch gathering can be a small event, not necessarily a big hall. It can be a church group, a youth club meeting, a school assembly, a small workshop, or even an office lunch session. The purpose is not the size. The purpose is clarity. I explain the problem the book solves, I teach one useful lesson from it, and I invite people to buy on the spot. If possible, I sign copies because signing adds personal value and creates memory.

Bulk activation means I use launch week to close at least one bulk deal. This could be a school order, an organization order, or an event package deal. Bulk orders create real momentum because they move many copies at once and create many readers who can later spread the book.

Daily placement means I visit two or three key points during the week and place copies: a shop, a stationery store, a school library, an office reception, or an event organizer. I do not try to place everywhere. I place where the buyer type already gathers.

Online launch week

My online launch week also has three pillars: the launch announcement, value posts, and direct follow-up.

The launch announcement is the main post or email that says the book is live. I keep it simple: what the book is, who it is for, and why it matters. I include the link and the clear promise. I do not write like a poet. I write like a publisher.

Value posts are short lessons taken from the book. I do not spend the whole week saying "buy my book." I spend the week giving small pieces that prove the book is useful. One day I share a pricing insight. Another day I share a distribution tip. Another day I share a common mistake and how to avoid it. Each post ends with a calm invitation: "If you want the full system, the book is available here."

Direct follow-up means I respond to comments and messages quickly during launch week. Launch week creates attention. Attention becomes sales when people feel seen. If someone asks a question and I answer well, they trust more. If someone says they bought, I thank them and guide them on how to use the book.

What I track daily during launch, and what I ignore

Tracking keeps me sober. It stops me from reacting to feelings. But tracking must be clean. If I track the wrong things, I will panic.

Here is what I track daily during launch week.

Offline daily tracking

Number of copies sold today
Number of copies placed today (consignment or shop placement)
Number of bulk leads contacted today
Number of bulk deals closed today
Cash collected today

Cash owed today
Stock remaining today

That is enough. I do not need complicated metrics. I need visibility.

Online daily tracking

Total sales today (ebook and print)
Page views or clicks to the listing from each channel I used
Email sign-ups if I offered a reader magnet or launch bonus
Direct messages or inquiries that signal buying intent

I keep it simple. The goal is to see what is working so I can repeat it.

Now, what do I ignore?

I ignore likes without meaning. Likes can be polite. They do not always lead to buying.

I ignore opinions from people who never buy books. Some people comment loudly but do not support. I do not build my emotions on them.

I ignore the urge to change everything daily. Launch week is short. If I keep rewriting the description and changing categories every day, I create instability. Small improvements are fine, but constant changes create chaos.

I ignore comparison with other authors. Their market is not my market. Their life is not my life. Comparison is a thief of discipline.

I also ignore any signal that is not tied to my goal. The goal is sales and reader relationships, not applause.

How I keep selling after the excitement fades

This is the heart of the chapter. After launch week, the business begins.

I keep selling by turning launch energy into a steady operating routine.

First, I do not stop promoting. I shift from launch mode to maintenance mode.

Launch mode is intense and daily.
Maintenance mode is steady and weekly.

In maintenance mode, I return to the rhythm I taught earlier: one main content anchor per week, a few smaller posts, and follow-up. The difference is that now I have proof. I have buyers. I have feedback. I can market with more confidence.

Second, I build partnerships after launch week.

Launch week often introduces the book to people, but partnerships are often closed after the week when leaders have time to decide. So I continue meetings with schools, organizations, and shops. I present the book as a solution. I offer bulk packages. I use receipts and clear terms.

Third, I collect and use feedback.

I ask buyers what chapter helped them most. I ask what they struggled with. I collect these answers and use them in future marketing because real reader language is stronger than my own marketing words.

If someone says, "This chapter on consignment saved me from being cheated," that sentence becomes a marketing line, not as a fake testimonial, but as a real signal of value.

Fourth, I build the catalog pathway.

After launch week, I do not treat the book like an only child. I plan the next title or the next related product. I link them. I guide readers. If I have other books, I point buyers to them. If I do not, I begin writing the next one. A catalog keeps selling because readers want more.

Fifth, I keep stock alive offline.

I schedule simple distribution rounds. For example, every two weeks I check shops and collect payments. Every month I visit key schools and organizations. This keeps the book visible in the real world. Offline sales are often slow, but they are steady if you maintain placement.

Sixth, I use email as the long engine.

After launch week, I send a thank-you email to new subscribers and buyers. I give them a simple "how to use this book" guide. Then I continue with weekly or biweekly teaching notes. This keeps the book present without constant social posting.

Finally, I measure the right horizon.

Launch week is seven days.
A book business is years.

So I ask, "What will keep this book selling for the next six months?" not "How do I make noise today?"

That question leads to steady actions: better partnerships, better positioning, better pathways, and better reader relationships.

Closing lesson

Launch week matters, but it is not the finish line. It is the beginning of proof.

If you want a launch that leads to a real business, keep it clean.

Prepare before you announce.
Execute with focus, not chaos.
Track what matters and ignore what does not.
Shift into a steady routine after the week ends.
Keep building channels, partnerships, and catalog pathways.

When you do that, the book does not die after the excitement fades. It becomes an asset that keeps earning, keeps spreading, and keeps serving, long after the loud week is over.

CHAPTER 15: TURNING ONE BOOK INTO A CATALOG THAT EARNS YEAR AFTER YEAR

A single book can change your life, but a catalog can stabilize your life. One book can bring a burst of sales, a season of attention, and a moment of pride. But one book can also bring pressure, because you start expecting it to pay every bill, solve every problem, and carry your whole identity. That is a dangerous weight to place on one title.

I learned that the book business becomes calm when I stop thinking in single titles and start thinking in catalog systems. A catalog is not just "many books." A catalog is a connected set of books that guide a reader from one outcome to the next. It is a pathway, not a pile.

In this chapter, I will teach series thinking, bundles, and reader pathways. I will show how I plan my next titles based on what the market already proved. Then I will explain how a catalog reduces pressure on any single book, which is one of the greatest gifts you can give yourself as a publisher.

Series thinking: the difference between random publishing and intentional publishing

Series thinking begins with a simple question.

If someone finishes this book and loves it, what should they read next?

If I cannot answer that, I am publishing randomly. Random publishing creates random sales. Random sales create random income. Random income creates stress.

Series thinking creates continuity. Continuity creates trust. Trust creates repeat buying.

Now, a "series" does not always mean a numbered series like Book 1, Book 2, Book 3. It can, but it does not have to. Series thinking means your books talk to each other. They share a clear theme, a consistent voice, and a connected purpose.

There are a few common series structures I use.

The step series.
This is where each book is a step in a process. Book 1 lays the foundation. Book 2 builds the system. Book 3 expands into advanced practice. Readers love this because it feels like progress.

The problem family.
This is where each book solves a specific problem inside one larger theme. For example, within "book business," one book might focus on writing discipline, another on offline distribution, another on online discoverability, another on pricing and printing math. Each book stands alone, but together they form a library of solutions.

The audience ladder.
This is where the same topic is taught to different groups. For example, "Book Business for Beginners," "Book Business for Teachers," "Book Business for NGOs," "Book Business for Christian Leaders," depending on

your world and your buyers. This can be powerful because it creates many entry points.

The format ladder.
This is where you expand formats: a main book, a workbook, a planner, a checklist guide, a case study book. Buyers love practical tools that help them apply the main lessons.

No matter which structure I choose, the goal is the same: give readers a reason to stay with me.

Reader pathways: guiding, not hoping

A reader pathway is the map I create for the buyer. It answers three questions.

Where should you start?
What should you read next?
What should you read when you are stuck in a specific area?

Most authors leave this to chance. They publish and hope the reader finds the next book. Hope is not a strategy. I build pathways deliberately.

I build pathways in three places.

Inside the book.
On the sales pages.
In email follow-up.

Inside the book, I include a simple "next step" note near the end. I do not make it long. I do not sound desperate. I simply guide.

"If you finished this book and you want to go deeper on offline sales, read this next."

This is powerful because the reader is already warmed up. They are already trusting me. They are already inside my world. That is the moment to guide.

On sales pages, I create "if you liked this, you will like that" sections. Again, it must be clean and clear.

In email follow-up, I send a message that helps the reader apply what they read, and then I point them to the next book that matches their stage.

This is how one book becomes a doorway, not a dead end.

Bundles: turning separate books into one stronger offer

Bundles are one of the simplest ways to increase value, increase order size, and serve the reader better.

A bundle is not a trick. A bundle is a curated set.

Instead of asking the reader to guess which book they need, I package books that belong together.

For example, in the book business theme, I might bundle:

The "Start" bundle: Book Business Map + Writing Discipline + Packaging and Pricing.
The "Sell" bundle: Offline Distribution + Online Discoverability + Launch Plan.
The "Scale" bundle: Catalog Building + Partnerships + Direct Sales.

Bundles work well offline and online.

Offline, bundles help at events and in shops because a buyer can buy two or three books at once and feel they got a deal. Bulk buyers also like bundles because they can buy a set for a program.

Online, bundles increase conversion when people want a complete system rather than a single book. If your pricing is clean, bundles can also raise your average revenue per customer.

I also bundle across formats.

A main book plus a workbook.
A main book plus a checklist.
A main book plus a planner.

This improves outcomes for readers, and better outcomes create better referrals. Referrals are the cheapest marketing you will ever get.

How I plan next titles based on what the market already proved

This is where many authors waste years. They write what they feel like writing, then they are shocked when the market does not respond. I do not build my catalog on shock. I build it on proof.

Proof means the market already showed me signals.

Signals can be:

People asked for a specific topic again and again.
A chapter in a book triggered many responses.
A post online got many questions.
A workshop topic caused people to buy quickly.
A certain audience group bought more than others.
A certain sales channel performed better than others.

I treat those signals as direction.

For example, if this book produces many questions about pricing and printing costs, that is a signal. It tells me the market is hungry for a deeper book or a practical workbook on publishing money math. I do not ignore that. I build the next title around it.

If people keep asking how to approach schools and organizations, that is a signal. It tells me a deeper "bulk sales and distribution" book will sell.

If people struggle with finishing their manuscripts, that is a signal. It tells me a writing discipline book will sell.

This is how I plan next titles. I do not guess. I listen and build.

I also use a simple method: the question list.

Every time someone asks me a question, I record it. After some time, I sort the questions into themes. The themes become books. The most repeated theme becomes the next book.

This is one of the most reliable catalog strategies because it is built on real demand, not imagination.

Another method I use is the "chapter expansion test."

If one chapter in a book could become a full book by itself, that is a sign the chapter contains a valuable system. I expand it.

For instance, a chapter on online discoverability could become a full book with deeper examples, keyword research practice, category strategy, description templates, and launch sequences.

A chapter on offline distribution could become a full book with scripts, proposal templates, consignment agreements, bulk pricing models, and tracking sheets.

Catalog building is often just expanding what already worked.

How a catalog reduces pressure on any single book

This is the emotional and business benefit of catalog thinking, and it is the part that keeps me alive.

A single book creates pressure because you are depending on one product. If sales slow, you panic. You start pushing too hard. You start doubting your gift. You start acting like the book failed, when it may simply be one piece in a larger system.

A catalog reduces pressure in five ways.

First, multiple entry points.
Different readers enter through different needs. One book might attract people who want discipline. Another attracts people who want marketing. Another attracts people who

want offline sales. All of them can lead into the same catalog.

Second, compounding visibility.
Each book promotes the others. The more books you have, the more chances buyers have to find you. One book might sell slowly, but ten books create a constant presence.

Third, stability across seasons.
Some topics sell better at certain times. A school-focused book may sell when terms begin. A goal-setting book may sell at the beginning of the year. A catalog gives you income in different seasons.

Fourth, stronger trust.
When readers see you have a body of work, they trust you more. They assume you are serious, not playing. That trust increases conversion and referrals.

Fifth, freedom to experiment.
With a catalog, you can test new ideas without risking everything. If one book underperforms, the catalog carries you. This keeps your mind calm and your creativity alive.

This is why I say a catalog is not just business. It is mental peace.

Practical catalog steps: how I build it without getting lost

Now I will give you a simple path, because catalog thinking can feel big.

Start with one core book that delivers a clear promise.

Then write the next book that naturally follows it. Do not jump. Build a pathway.

Keep consistent branding so readers recognize the family.

Create a simple "start here" guide on your website or in your book's back matter.

Bundle related books once you have at least two or three that truly belong together.

Collect feedback and questions, and let demand shape your next titles.

This is the path. It is not glamorous, but it works.

Closing lesson

A catalog is the publisher's long game. It turns one win into many wins. It turns one book into a library. It turns your work into a system that keeps earning while you write the next piece.

If you want books to earn year after year, stop treating each title like a separate project. Treat each title like a brick in a house.

Series thinking gives structure.
Bundles increase value and order size.
Reader pathways create repeat buyers.
Market proof guides your next titles.
Catalog building reduces pressure and creates stability.

When you build like this, you stop fearing slow weeks. You stop worshiping launch week. You stop begging for attention. You become what you already are: a publisher building assets that serve people and sustain a life of writing.

CHAPTER 16: HANDLING DOUBT, CRITICISM, AND ENVY WITHOUT LOSING FOCUS

If you publish seriously, you will meet three enemies that do not always show their faces clearly. Doubt will rise inside you. Criticism will come from outside you. Envy will move around you. None of these are new. They are part of any visible work. But books make it sharper because publishing is public. People can see your name on a cover. They can see you selling. They can see you speaking. They can see you building something. And when people see you building, they react.

I used to think the main battle was writing. I later learned that the main battle is staying steady. A book business is not destroyed only by bad printing or weak marketing. Many book businesses are destroyed by emotional turbulence. The author gets tired of comments. The author loses courage. The author starts explaining themselves too much. The author gets dragged into fights. The author stops publishing. And once you stop publishing, the business stops breathing.

So in this chapter I will teach how I handle doubt, criticism, and envy without losing focus. I will teach how I respond with results, not arguments. I will show how I build credibility through consistency, quality, and service. Then I will explain how I protect my mission while staying commercially smart, because mission without strategy becomes frustration, and strategy without mission becomes emptiness.

Doubt: the voice that tries to stop the work before it grows

Doubt is not always loud. Sometimes it sounds like wisdom. It says things like:

"Who will buy this?"
"You are not qualified."
"You are wasting time."
"People do not read here."
"You will fail."
"Your writing is not good enough."
"Just wait until life is stable."

Doubt loves delay. Doubt loves perfectionism. Doubt loves endless planning. Doubt loves comparing you to people who have different lives.

I do not try to destroy doubt by emotion. I destroy doubt by systems.

When doubt rises, I return to the basics.

I ask: what is my daily minimum?
I ask: what is my next small publishing action?
I ask: what is one piece of service I can give today?

Doubt dies when work moves.

I also use a simple truth that protects me.

I do not need everyone to believe in me. I only need to keep publishing and keep serving.

A book business is not built by one big moment of courage. It is built by a thousand small acts of discipline. Doubt cannot survive where discipline is steady.

I also keep proof close. Proof is not praise. Proof is evidence.

Proof is the email from a reader who says the book helped.
Proof is the school that bought 50 copies.
Proof is the shop that reordered.
Proof is the friend who used a method from my book and got results.

When doubt rises, I read proof. Not to inflate ego, but to remember that the work is real.

Criticism: separating feedback from noise

Criticism is not one thing. There is useful criticism and there is noisy criticism.

Useful criticism helps me improve.
Noisy criticism tries to shame me.

A wise publisher learns the difference quickly.

Useful criticism usually sounds specific and calm.

"The formatting was hard to read in Chapter 3."
"The title made me expect a different focus."
"The cover looks like fiction but the book is business."
"I wish there were more examples on pricing."

That kind of feedback is gold because it shows me how to serve readers better. I do not argue with it. I thank the person. I fix what I can. I improve the next edition. I learn.

Noisy criticism usually sounds vague, personal, and emotional.

"This is rubbish."
"You are just trying to make money."
"Who do you think you are?"
"You think you are better than us."
"Stop pretending you are a publisher."

That kind of criticism is not about the book. It is about the person's discomfort. If I argue with it, I lose time and peace. I also advertise the critic.

So I built a rule.

I accept useful criticism as a tool.
I ignore noisy criticism as a distraction.

This rule saved me years.

Now let me explain how I respond with results, not arguments, because this is the center of the chapter.

How I respond with results, not arguments

Arguments feel like action, but they are usually a trap. Arguments drain energy. Arguments rarely change minds. Arguments often turn your attention away from the work that would actually prove your point.

When someone criticizes my work unfairly, my first instinct is to explain myself. But I learned that explanation is often the wrong response. If I explain too much, I look unsure. If I defend too much, I look guilty. If I fight, I look emotional. None of these build a brand.

So I respond with results.

Results are quiet, but they are loud in the long run.

Instead of arguing, I publish the next book.
Instead of replying to insults, I improve the cover and the interior.
Instead of fighting rumors, I deliver a workshop that helps real people.
Instead of proving myself with words, I prove myself with service.

This approach protects my focus and makes my critics irrelevant over time.

Sometimes I do respond in words, but only with discipline.

If a criticism is public and could mislead buyers, I respond briefly, respectfully, and once. Then I stop.

I say something like, "Thank you for your comment. This book is designed to help readers do X. If you are looking for Y, it may not be a fit."

That is all. No fight. No pride. No endless thread.

I also keep my emotions out of the marketplace. If someone leaves a negative review, I do not attack them. I do not beg them. I learn from it if it is useful. If it is noise, I leave it.

A publisher who argues with reviewers looks unstable. A publisher who stays calm looks trustworthy.

Envy: the hidden tax of progress

Envy is the hardest enemy because it hides behind friendship, family, community expectations, and even religious language. Envy is not always open hatred. Sometimes it is subtle.

It shows up as jokes about your ambition.
It shows up as constant discouragement.
It shows up as people questioning your motives.
It shows up as people demanding free copies as a test of loyalty.
It shows up as people spreading stories when you refuse to be controlled.

Envy often appears when you move from being ordinary to being productive. Not because your success harms them, but because it reminds them of what they have not done.

I learned not to hate people for envy. Many people do not even know they are envious. They are just uncomfortable. But I also learned not to let envy shape my decisions.

So I set boundaries.

I do not give free copies to people who only want to consume without respect.
I do give review copies strategically when it serves the

business and the mission.
I do not lower my price to satisfy someone's jealousy.
I do create occasional discounts for real readers who need access, but that is my decision, not social pressure.

Envy wants to pull you back into the crowd. The crowd is comfortable because no one stands out. But the crowd is also where dreams die quietly. I refuse to die quietly.

How I build credibility through consistency, quality, and service

Credibility is not a speech. Credibility is a pattern.

People trust what they see repeatedly.

If you publish one book and disappear, people may praise you, but they will not trust you as a serious publisher.

If you publish consistently, improve each release, and serve readers, trust grows. Trust becomes credibility.

So I build credibility in three ways.

Consistency.
I keep publishing. I keep showing up. I keep teaching. I keep meeting bulk buyers. I keep distributing. Even when sales fluctuate, I keep moving. Consistency makes people stop doubting your seriousness.

Quality.
I improve packaging. I improve editing. I improve formatting. I improve covers. I improve descriptions. I fix errors. I update editions when needed. Quality makes

people respect your work even if they do not like you personally.

Service.
I answer questions. I guide readers. I create tools. I offer workshops. I follow up after sales. I help schools deploy books. I treat buyers with respect. Service makes people advocate for you, because they feel you care.

These three create credibility in a way that arguments never can.

How I protect my mission while staying commercially smart

Some people act like mission and money cannot sit together. They think if you care about people, you must be poor. That is false, and it is also dangerous. A broke mission becomes a wounded mission. You cannot print books without money. You cannot travel to events without money. You cannot reinvest without money. You cannot build a catalog without money.

So I protect my mission by being commercially smart.

Here is how.

I price for sustainability, not for applause.
If I underprice to look humble, I will not be able to reprint. Then the mission dies.

I reinvest profits intentionally.
I use profits to print the next batch, improve the cover, upgrade editing, build direct sales, and support distribution.

I choose channels that match the mission.
If my mission includes reaching people offline, I do not rely only on online marketplaces. I build school and organization channels too.

I keep the message clear.
Commercially smart does not mean manipulating people. It means communicating the promise clearly so the right buyer can decide quickly.

I protect my time.
If I let criticism and envy drag me into endless battles, my mission suffers because the work slows.

I also keep my ethics clean.

I do not promise income results I cannot guarantee.
I do not exaggerate.
I do not use fake testimonials.
I do not attack competitors.
I do not steal content.
I do not beg.

This is part of integrity. Integrity is not only moral. It is commercial intelligence. When buyers sense integrity, they trust you and buy with less resistance.

The practical posture I keep

To close this chapter, I want to leave you with a posture I keep as a publisher.

I stay humble enough to learn.
I stay firm enough to keep publishing.
I stay calm enough to ignore noise.

I stay disciplined enough to let results speak.
I stay wise enough to protect the business side so the mission can live.

Doubt will come.
Criticism will come.
Envy will come.

But none of them have the right to stop the work.

My response is not to shout. My response is to build.

I publish again.
I serve again.
I improve again.
I distribute again.

And over time, the noise fades, the work remains, and the catalog stands like evidence that I did not waste my life arguing when I could have been producing.

CHAPTER 17: TRAINING OTHERS AND MULTIPLYING THE MARKET

When I first started treating books as a business, I thought the market was fixed. I thought there were only a few buyers, only a few readers, and only a few people willing to pay. That belief makes an author selfish and fearful. It makes you protect your ideas like food in a famine. It makes you see other writers as threats. It makes you hoard, hide, and compete in small circles.

Then I learned a truth that changed how I build.

The market is not fixed. The market can be grown.

Readers are made, not only found.
Buyers are trained, not only chased.
Writers are developed, not only born.

This is why training others matters. Mentoring and workshops do more than help people. They multiply the market. They create new readers who understand why books matter. They create new writers who become producers, not just consumers. They create a community that supports buying habits. They also strengthen my own credibility and sales, not by manipulation, but by building trust and capability in the people around me.

In this chapter, I will teach how mentoring and workshops grow both community and sales. I will show how I use events to create readers and new writers. Then I will explain why building other authors is not competition but market expansion, because that is the mindset that turns a lonely author into a true publisher-leader.

Why training grows the book business

Let me say it plainly.

If you want to sell books in a place where reading is weak, you must strengthen reading.
If you want to sell books in a place where buying habits are inconsistent, you must normalize buying books.
If you want to build a long-term publishing ecosystem, you must build more producers.

Training is the fastest way I know to do that.

When I teach people how to read better, write better, or publish better, I create a chain reaction.

People become more interested in books.
People start seeing books as tools, not decorations.
People start buying books because they understand how books can change their skills and outcomes.
People start recommending books because they can speak about them with clarity.
Some people become writers, and writers create more books, and more books create more readers.

This is not theory. I have watched it happen. A single workshop can turn a room of silent listeners into a circle of readers who now want to own a book, not just borrow it.

Training also solves a problem that kills many authors: the isolation problem.

When you publish alone and sell alone, you burn out.
When you train others, you build a community.

Community carries you when motivation is low. Community also becomes your distribution network because people who learn from you often become your ambassadors.

Mentoring and workshops that grow both community and sales

Now let us talk about mentoring and workshops in a practical way. Many people hear "workshop" and imagine a big hotel hall, fancy banners, microphones, and heavy budgets. That can happen, but it is not required.

A workshop is simply a structured learning session that produces a clear outcome.

A mentoring relationship is simply a guided support path that helps someone improve over time.

Both can be built small and still be powerful.

The key is that training must be outcome-based, not talk-based.

If I run a workshop and people leave with nothing concrete, they will clap and forget. If people leave with a finished outline, a clear publishing plan, a clean book description, or a daily writing system, they remember. They also trust.

Trust is what turns learning into sales.

So I design training with three elements.

A clear promise.
A simple method.
A tangible output.

For example, a workshop promise might be:
"By the end of this session, you will have a one-page book business map for your next 90 days."

The method might be:
Create, package, distribute, sell, repeat.

The tangible output might be:
A completed worksheet that each participant can use immediately.

Now, how does this grow sales?

First, training creates a reason for people to buy the book. Instead of me saying, "Buy my book," the workshop makes the buyer say, "I need the full system."

Second, training creates authority without bragging. When people see you teach clearly, they trust you. They do not need social proof from far away. They have lived proof.

Third, training creates groups of buyers.
A workshop can sell 20 copies in one room. That is not random selling. That is organized selling.

Fourth, training creates repeat buyers.
If someone learns from me once and gets results, they want the next level. That is why I design workshops as a pathway, not as a one-time event.

The workshop ladder: creating multiple levels

To keep training sustainable, I build a simple ladder.

Intro workshop.
This is basic, cheap or accessible, and focused on one outcome.

Intermediate workshop.
This is deeper, more practical, and includes implementation support.

Advanced workshop or mentorship.
This is personalized help, higher value, and usually limited seats.

This ladder allows different people to join at different levels. It also protects my time. Not everyone needs personal mentoring. Many people only need a clear system and some accountability. The ladder serves both groups.

How I use events to create readers and new writers

Events are not only for selling. Events are for shaping culture.

If you want books to sell, you must make books visible, respected, and discussed. Events do that. But the event must be designed well.

I use events for three main purposes.

Reader creation events.
These are designed to make people fall in love with reading again.

Writer creation events.
These are designed to help people see that writing is possible for them, and that publishing is not only for outsiders.

Publishing business events.
These are designed to help serious authors turn their books into assets.

Now let me show you the structure I use for an event that creates both readers and writers.

I open with a story.
Not a long story. A short one that shows why books matter. It can be a story of how a book helped me survive a hard season, or how reading opened my mind, or how writing turned pain into meaning. The story creates emotional permission. People relax. They listen.

Then I teach one clear lesson.
For example, I might teach the difference between a manuscript and a product, or the cycle of create, package, distribute, sell, repeat. The lesson gives intellectual clarity.

Then I do a small exercise.
This is where transformation happens.

If it is a reader event, the exercise might be:
"Write down one problem you want to solve in your life right now, and one book topic that could help."

If it is a writer event, the exercise might be:
"Write your book promise in one sentence."

If it is a publishing event, the exercise might be:
"Choose one channel where your buyers gather and write a plan to place the book there this month."

Then I invite action.
Action might be buying the book, joining the next workshop, or joining a reading club.

Then I close with a pathway.
"Start here. Then do this next. Then come back for this next step."

This is how events become engines, not entertainment.

Using events to build reading habits

Let me be honest about a real-world problem. In many places, people do not buy books because they do not have the habit. They may love the idea of books, but habit is stronger than admiration. So I use events to build habit.

I create small reading challenges.
A seven-day reading plan.
A 30-day reading challenge.
A book club with weekly meetings.

When people participate, they stop seeing reading as a school punishment and start seeing reading as a tool. That shift creates demand for books.

I also make buying books socially normal.

When a group buys together, buying becomes belonging. People like belonging. This is not manipulation. It is how humans work. A culture is built by shared behavior.

Using events to create new writers

Now, creating new writers is even more powerful because writers become nodes in the market.

A writer does not only buy one book. A writer buys editing support, cover design, formatting, training, and often many other books. Writers also become teachers in their own circles. They create content that brings more people into reading.

So when I run writer creation events, I do not begin with "write a novel." I begin with "write a useful book." That is easier and more practical.

I teach people to start with a problem.

What do you know that can help someone?
What have you survived that can teach a lesson?
What skill can you explain simply?
What process can you show step by step?

Then I teach structure.

Title.
Promise.
Audience.
Outline.
Draft plan.

I also teach them to finish. Many people start, few finish. If I can help someone finish, they become confident. Confidence multiplies output.

Once someone finishes their first book, they become a believer. Believers spread belief. That is how markets expand.

Why building other authors is not competition but market expansion

Now let us address the fear that sits in many authors.

"If I train other writers, they will compete with me."

This fear is understandable, but it is also small-market thinking.

Competition only scares you when you believe the market is tiny and fixed. When you understand that the market can grow, you see that other authors are not enemies. They are builders of demand.

Here is why.

More authors create more books.
More books create more readers.
More readers create more buyers.
More buyers create stronger bookshops, stronger events, stronger reading clubs, stronger distribution channels.
Stronger channels benefit everyone.

If you are the person helping build those channels, your position becomes stronger, not weaker.

Also, the truth is this: not every author serves the same audience, even if the topic overlaps. People choose teachers based on voice, trust, values, and style. If I focus on quality and service, I will not be replaced by someone who learned the basics from me. Instead, that person becomes part of the ecosystem.

There is another important point.

When you build other authors, you build allies.

Allies promote your work.
Allies invite you to events.
Allies recommend you for partnerships.
Allies become your distribution network.

This is how publishing becomes bigger than one person.

The commercial intelligence in training others

Let me also show you why this is commercially smart, not only morally good.

Training creates a pipeline.

From the public event, some people buy a book.
From the book, some people join the email list.
From the email list, some people join a workshop.
From the workshop, some people join mentorship.
From mentorship, some people publish, and their success becomes a story that attracts more learners.

This pipeline grows community and revenue in a way that does not depend on constant social posting.

It also reduces marketing stress, because the market begins to market itself through word of mouth.

Protecting integrity while training and selling

Now, training can become exploitative if done poorly. I refuse that. I do not use training to trap people in endless upsells. I use training to help people. If I help them, some will naturally buy more because they want deeper support.

So I keep integrity rules.

I set clear expectations about what the workshop includes.
I price fairly.
I deliver what I promised.
I respect people's time.
I never shame anyone for not buying.
I give enough value that even a person who buys nothing still leaves better than they came.

This integrity is not only moral. It builds trust, and trust is the strongest marketing.

Closing lesson

Training others is one of the highest forms of publishing leadership. It multiplies the market instead of fighting over small pieces. It turns reading into habit, writing into possibility, and buying into normal behavior.

Mentoring and workshops grow community and sales because they produce outcomes and trust.
Events create readers and new writers because they make books visible and practical.
Building other authors is not competition, it is market expansion, because more producers create more demand and stronger channels.

So I do not fear training others. I embrace it.

I build readers.
I build writers.
I build channels.
I build a culture.

And when the culture grows, the market grows, and books stop being a lonely struggle. They become a shared economy of learning, meaning, and sustainable work.

CHAPTER 18: THE LONG GAME, BUILDING A REAL PUBLISHING BUSINESS

A publishing business becomes real when it stops depending on my mood and starts depending on systems. In the early stages, I can carry everything with energy. I can write, edit, design, print, sell, deliver, promote, collect payments, and follow up by myself. That phase feels heroic, but it is also fragile. If I get sick, if my schedule breaks, if my life shifts, the whole thing slows down. That is not a business yet. That is a strong person working hard.

The long game is different. The long game is building something that can keep running even when my energy is not at its peak. It is building something that can outlive my best seasons and still serve people with dignity. It is building a publishing operation that is stable, ethical, and scalable, without becoming cold or greedy.

In this chapter, I will teach systems: documentation, roles, partners, and scaling with integrity. I will show how I expand formats and rights over time. Then I will explain how I build something that can outlive my energy and still serve people, because that is the difference between a hustle and a legacy.

Systems: turning talent into an operation

A system is simply a repeatable way of producing an outcome. If I can repeat it, I can teach it. If I can teach it, I can delegate it. If I can delegate it, I can scale it.

Most authors do not scale because everything lives in their head. They are brilliant, but their brilliance is not documented. That means no one can help without constantly asking them. That drains the author, and the author becomes the bottleneck.

So I started documenting my publishing system. Not with fancy language. With simple steps and checklists.

Documentation is not bureaucracy. Documentation is freedom.

When I document, I create a "how we do things here" guide. Even if "we" is just me today, it becomes "we" tomorrow when I bring in help.

What do I document?

I document the whole book production pipeline.

Manuscript checklist.
Editing stages checklist.
Formatting checklist for ebook and print.
Cover brief template.
Metadata checklist.
Upload checklist.
Proofing checklist.
Launch checklist.
Offline distribution checklist.
Bulk sales proposal template.
Consignment agreement template.
Receipt and invoice template.
Weekly marketing routine checklist.
Customer follow-up scripts.

These are not complicated documents. They can be one page each. But they hold my business steady.

I also document standards.

Brand standards: how covers should look, how titles should be structured, how series should stay consistent.
Quality standards: minimum editing level, formatting cleanliness, proofing rules.
Customer standards: response time, refund policy, delivery rules, professionalism.

Standards protect integrity because they make quality predictable. When quality is predictable, people trust you more.

Roles: building a small team without losing control

In the long game, I cannot do everything myself. But I also cannot outsource blindly. If I hand over the core thinking, the brand becomes confused. If I keep the core thinking and delegate supporting tasks, the business grows while the mission stays intact.

So I define roles.

In early stages, I keep these roles in my mind even if one person is doing them.

Publisher role.
This is strategic leadership. Choosing projects, defining the promise, setting pricing, selecting channels, protecting the brand.

Editor role.
This is polishing clarity and correctness. It can be professional editing, or a trusted reader team, or both.

Designer role.
Cover design, interior layout, visual consistency.

Production role.
File preparation, uploads, proof coordination, print management.

Sales and distribution role.
Shop placement, bulk deals, event sales, inventory tracking.

Marketing role.
Content repurposing, posting routines, email, partnerships.

Admin role.
Receipts, invoices, payment tracking, record keeping.

When I name the roles, I can decide what to delegate first.

I usually delegate what drains me most while still protecting quality.

Some authors delegate marketing first. Some delegate formatting. Some delegate delivery and admin. I decide based on where my time is bleeding.

But I keep two roles close to my chest for a long time: publisher role and brand voice. These are the identity of the business.

Partners: scaling without hiring a full staff

Many authors think scaling requires hiring employees. Not always. Partners can scale you faster and with less risk.

A partner is someone who shares distribution or value creation with you.

There are distribution partners and service partners.

Distribution partners are:
Bookshops and stationery shops.
School networks and training centers.
Church networks and ministries.
NGOs and program leaders.
Event organizers.
Libraries and reading clubs.
Corporate training departments.

Service partners are:
Editors.
Designers.
Printers.
Logistics people.
Digital assistants.
Web developers.
Accountants.

Partners allow you to scale in a modular way. You do not need to own everything. You need to control the system and choose reliable relationships.

The rule with partners is simple.

Clarity protects relationships.
Clear terms prevent misunderstanding.

So I keep agreements simple and written. I do not rely on memory. I rely on documents.

Scaling with integrity: growth that does not poison the mission

Scaling is dangerous when it becomes obsession with money. Money is necessary, but obsession twists the heart and ruins trust.

So I scale with integrity.

Integrity in publishing means:

I do not mislead buyers with exaggerated promises.
I do not copy others and pretend it is mine.
I do not use fake reviews.
I do not manipulate readers with guilt.
I do not chase trends that contradict my values.
I pay partners fairly.
I honor agreements.
I keep receipts and accountability.
I maintain quality even when volume rises.

Integrity is not a charity posture. Integrity is a business advantage. People can sense when you are clean. Clean brands last longer.

Now I will show you how I expand formats and rights over time, because this is one of the strongest long-game strategies.

Expanding formats over time: making one idea work harder

A single manuscript can live in multiple formats. Many authors leave money and impact on the table because they publish only one version and stop.

I expand formats gradually, not all at once.

I start with the core format that matches my buyer.

If my buyers are online and global, ebook and print-on-demand paperback might come first.
If my buyers are offline and local, paperback might come first with an ebook later.
If my buyers prefer listening, audio can become important later.

Then I expand.

From one core book, I can create:

A workbook.
A guided journal.
A planner.
A short field guide edition.
A course outline.
A workshop curriculum.
A speaking program.
A translated edition for another language market.
An audiobook.
A hardcover collector edition.
A bundle set.

Each format serves different buyer needs. Some people want to read. Some want to apply. Some want to listen. Some want to gift. Some want a classroom tool.

The key is not to create formats for ego. I create formats for outcomes.

If readers struggle to apply, I create a workbook.
If readers want structure, I create a planner.
If organizations want training material, I create a curriculum.
If busy people want audio, I create an audiobook.

This is how one book becomes a product family.

Expanding rights over time: turning books into assets beyond sales

Rights are one of the most ignored parts of publishing by new authors. But rights are where long-term value often lives.

When I own my rights, I have options.

I can license translations.
I can license audio production.
I can license excerpts to institutions.
I can sell bulk rights for training programs.
I can create special editions for partners.
I can negotiate distribution deals without losing ownership.

The long game is keeping my rights clean and flexible.

This is why I read contracts carefully. I do not sign away rights casually. I do not give exclusive control unless the deal truly earns it.

Owning rights is not greed. It is stewardship. If I lose my rights, I lose my ability to serve the market in new ways later.

Building something that can outlive my energy and still serve people

Now let me talk about the deepest part of the chapter.

Outliving my energy does not mean I plan to stop writing. It means I plan for seasons when I am tired, busy, or limited. It means the business should not collapse when my life shifts.

So I build three forms of durability.

Durability through documentation.
If the system is written, others can follow it.

Durability through catalog.
If the catalog is strong, sales can continue even when I am not promoting daily.

Durability through community.
If I trained readers and writers, the ecosystem continues through people, not just through me.

I also build durability through a simple operational center.

A central website or store.
An email list.

A clear catalog page.
A consistent brand identity.
A basic CRM style record of bulk buyers and partners.
A repeatable production schedule.

These form the spine of the business.

Then I build a "minimum viable week" that can keep the business alive even in hard seasons.

One email.
One piece of content.
One follow-up block.
One distribution check-in.
One writing block.

This minimum week keeps the engine warm. Then, when energy returns, I accelerate.

This is how I build something that lasts.

A teaching example to make it real

Let me use a simple example.

Deng is a young writer I mentored. He learns my system. He publishes his first book. His success creates excitement in his circle. That circle now respects books more. They buy his book, and they also ask about mine. Deng invites me to speak at his school. I sell 50 copies. Another teacher hears about it and orders 100 copies for her class.

Now imagine that multiplied by ten writers and ten circles. That is market expansion. That is durability. Even if I have a quiet month, the ecosystem is still moving. That is the long game.

Closing lesson

A real publishing business is not built by bursts. It is built by systems.

Documentation turns your knowledge into repeatable operations.
Roles turn your effort into a team structure.
Partners turn your reach into channels.
Integrity keeps growth clean and trustworthy.
Formats make one idea serve more people in more ways.
Rights keep your options open as markets change.
Catalog and community create durability that can outlive your best energy.

This is how I build a publishing business that lasts. Not only for money, but for service. Not only for today, but for years. Not only to sell books, but to create a living culture where books are tools, readers are builders, writers are producers, and the work keeps moving even when I am quiet.

APPENDICES: COPY-READY BUSINESS TOOLS

These appendices are meant to be used, not admired. Copy them into a notebook, a document, or a spreadsheet. Print them and keep them in your publishing folder. Use them when you are tired. Use them when you are confused. Use them when you are tempted to guess instead of plan.

A book business becomes calm when the tools are ready before the pressure comes.

APPENDIX A: MY BOOK BUSINESS ONE-PAGE PLAN TEMPLATE

Book title:
Subtitle:
Book type: (guide, memoir, workbook, fiction, devotional, manual, etc.)
Format plan: (ebook, paperback, hardcover, audio, workbook, bundle)

1. THE BUYER

Primary buyer (one sentence):
Example: "A busy adult who wants to build a real book income using simple systems."

Secondary buyer (optional):
Example: "A teacher, pastor, or program leader who wants a training tool."

Where does this buyer gather offline?
List 5 places:
1.
2.
3.
4.
5.

Where does this buyer gather online?
List 5 places:
1.
2.

3.
4.
5.

2. THE PROMISE

The promise statement (one sentence):
"After reading this book, you will be able to
_____."

What problem does it solve?
Write the problem in the buyer's words:
"Right now I struggle with
_____."

What outcome does the reader want?
"By the end, I want _____."

3. THE PRODUCT

What is inside (bullet outline of what the reader will learn):

- _____
- _____
- _____
- _____
- _____

Proof or credibility (what makes you qualified):

- lived experience:
- results you have:
- teaching/work background:
- examples or case studies:

4. THE CHANNELS

Offline channels I will activate first:

- Channel 1:
- Channel 2:
- Channel 3:

Online channels I will activate first:

- Channel 1:
- Channel 2:
- Channel 3:

Direct sales plan:
Where will I sell directly? (website, WhatsApp, email, events, etc.)

- _____

5. THE LAUNCH

Launch date:
Launch week target (copies or revenue target):
Offline event plan (place and date):
Online announcement plan (where and when):

6. THE NUMBERS

Estimated unit cost per book:
Retail price:
Wholesale price:
Expected margin per unit:
Break-even units (how many copies I must sell to recover total costs):

7. THE NEXT STEP

What is the next book in the pathway?
Title or topic:
Why this is next:
Expected buyer overlap:

APPENDIX B: PRICING AND MARGIN CALCULATOR

Use this calculator for both local printing and platform printing.

1. UNIT COST (PER COPY)

Printing cost per copy:
Cover finishing cost per copy (if separate):
Shipping cost per copy (if any):
Packaging cost per copy:
Transaction cost per copy (if any):
Total unit cost per copy (A) = sum of the above

A = _____

2. RETAIL PRICING

Retail selling price (B) = _____

Retail gross profit per copy (C) = B - A

C = _____

Retail gross margin percent (D) = (C / B) x 100

D = _____ %

3. WHOLESALE PRICING

Wholesale discount percent (example: 30% or 40%) = _____

Wholesale price (E) = B x (1 - discount)

E = _____

Wholesale gross profit per copy (F) = E - A

F = _____

Wholesale gross margin percent (G) = (F / E) x 100

G = _____ %

4. CONSIGNMENT PRICING

Consignment commission percent to seller (example: 20% or 30%) = _____

Your payout per copy (H) = B x (1 - commission)

H = _____

Consignment gross profit per copy (I) = H - A

I = _____

5. BREAK-EVEN

Total fixed costs for this release (editing + cover design + ISBN + proofs + travel + launch costs + ads if any) = _____

Break-even units retail (J) = fixed costs / C

J = _____ copies

Break-even units wholesale (K) = fixed costs / F

K = _____ copies

APPENDIX C: PRINT-RUN AND INVENTORY TRACKER

Print Run ID:
Book title:
Print date:
Printer:
Unit cost:
Total copies printed:
Total cost:

INVENTORY MOVEMENT LOG

Date	Movement type (printed / delivered / sold / consigned / returned / damaged)	Quantity	Channel (shop/school/event/online/direct)	Price per unit	Total	Payment status (paid/owed)	Notes

INVENTORY SUMMARY

Starting stock:
Added stock (new print runs):
Total available:
Total sold:
Total placed on consignment:
Total returned:
Total damaged/lost:
Ending stock (should match physical count):

APPENDIX D: METADATA WORKSHEET (TITLE PROMISE, DESCRIPTION BLOCKS, KEYWORDS, CATEGORIES)

1. TITLE + SUBTITLE

Working title:
Subtitle:
Book type:
Target reader (one sentence):

2. PROMISE STATEMENT

Promise statement (one sentence):
"After reading this book, you will be able to _____."

3. DESCRIPTION BLOCKS (COPY-READY)

Block 1: Hook + problem (2–4 lines)
Write the buyer's pain clearly:

_____
_____

Block 2: Promise + transformation (2–4 lines)
What changes for them?

_____
_____

Block 3: What's inside (list of benefits or key sections)

- _____
- _____

- _____
- _____
- _____

Block 4: Who it's for (and who it's not for)
This book is for:

_____

This book is not for:

_____

Block 5: Call to action (simple and direct)

_____

4. KEYWORDS (BUYER LANGUAGE)

Main topic keywords (5–10):
1.
2.
3.
4.
5.
6.
7.
8.
9.
10.

Outcome keywords (5–10):
1.
2.
3.

4.
5.
6.
7.
8.
9.
10.

Method keywords (5–10):
1.
2.
3.
4.
5.
6.
7.
8.
9.
10.

5. CATEGORIES

Primary categories (2–3):
1.
2.
3.

Secondary categories (2–3):
1.
2.
3.

Competing books I resemble (for positioning):
1.

2.
3.

APPENDIX E: OFFLINE SALES SCRIPTS (SCHOOLS, CHURCHES, OFFICES, SHOPS)

These scripts are meant to be adapted. Keep the structure. Change the words to match your voice.

1. SCHOOL SCRIPT (HEAD TEACHER OR ACADEMIC DIRECTOR)

Greeting:
"Good morning. My name is Panyim. I'm a publisher and I wrote a book that helps students with _____."

Purpose:
"I'm not here to waste your time. I'm here because your students face _____, and this book provides a practical system to improve _____."

Fit and outcome:
"The book is designed for _____ level. It helps students achieve _____ within _____."

Offer:
"I'd like to propose a bulk package for a reading club or classroom program. For example, 30 copies for a club, or 100 copies for a grade level. I can also do a one-hour orientation session for students on how to use the book."

Next step:
"If you are open, we can start with a small pilot. What would be the best person to coordinate with on purchasing and scheduling?"

2. CHURCH SCRIPT (PASTOR OR LEADER)

Greeting:
"Pastor, thank you for your time. I wrote a book that supports believers and leaders by helping them _____."

Purpose:
"This is not just a book to read. It's a tool for discipleship and growth."

Offer:
"I'd like to supply copies for a small group, youth fellowship, or leadership training. We can do bulk pricing, and I can also give a short teaching session after a service or during a training day."

Next step:
"Who oversees church training programs or book orders so I can follow the right process?"

3. OFFICE/ORGANIZATION SCRIPT (HR, PROGRAM MANAGER, DIRECTOR)

Greeting:
"Hello. I'm Panyim. I work with books as training tools. I noticed your organization focuses on _____."

Purpose:
"I wrote a book that helps people improve _____ with a practical step-by-step method."

Offer:
"I'd like to propose a bulk supply for your team or program participants, plus a short workshop to help them apply it."

Proof:
"I can share a one-page outline of outcomes and how the book can be used inside your program."

Next step:
"What is your procurement process, and who signs off on training materials?"

4. SHOP SCRIPT (BOOKSHOP OR STATIONERY)

Greeting:
"Hello. I'm a local publisher. I'd like to place this book here because customers who buy _____ often ask for _____."

Terms:
"We can do wholesale or consignment. Wholesale means you buy at a discount and resell. Consignment means you pay after sales. Either way, we keep clear records and reconcile on a set date."

Small start:
"Let's start with 5–10 copies and see how it moves. If it sells, I restock fast."

Next step:
"What terms do you prefer, and when do you normally reconcile stock and payments?"

APPENDIX F: WHOLESALE AND CONSIGNMENT TERMS TEMPLATE

Document title: Book Supply Agreement
Date:
Supplier (Author/Publisher):
Buyer/Outlet:
Location:
Contact person:
Phone/email:

Book title:
Format: (paperback/hardcover)
Retail price per copy:
Quantity:

Option A: Wholesale Terms
Wholesale price per copy:
Total amount:
Payment terms: (full upfront / deposit + balance date)
Delivery date:
Returns policy: (yes/no, conditions)
Damage policy: (who carries damage)

Option B: Consignment Terms
Quantity placed:
Retail price per copy:
Outlet commission percent:
Supplier payout per copy:
Reconciliation schedule: (every 2 weeks / monthly)
Payment due date after reconciliation:

Loss/damage responsibility:
Return policy at end of term:
Consignment term start date:
Consignment term end date:

Signatures:
Supplier:
Outlet:
Date:

APPENDIX G: LAUNCH CHECKLIST (OFFLINE AND ONLINE)

Pre-launch (2–4 weeks before)
Manuscript final proof done
Cover final and tested as thumbnail
Interior formatted and checked
ISBN/metadata ready (if used)
Print proof approved
Stock ordered or POD ready
Pricing set (retail, wholesale, consignment)
Sales pages written (marketplace + direct sales)
Email list signup or reader offer prepared
Launch messages drafted (core message + versions)
Partners contacted (shops, schools, organizations)
Event venue confirmed (if any)
Receipts/invoice templates ready

Launch week (day-by-day)
Day 1: Announcement + first value lesson + direct follow-up
Day 2: Second value lesson + partner check-in + distribution placement
Day 3: Event or live session + bulk proposal follow-up
Day 4: Reader story/testimonial request + restock where

needed
Day 5: Third value lesson + email reminder + shop reconciliation check
Day 6: Direct sales push + small discount or bundle offer (optional)
Day 7: Thank-you post + "how to use the book" guidance + next-step pathway

Post-launch (weeks 2–6)
Collect feedback and reviews (without pressure)
Update description if clarity is needed
Strengthen pathways to other books
Continue weekly marketing routine
Follow up on bulk leads
Restock strong channels
Track monthly scorecard

APPENDIX H: MONTHLY SCORECARD (SALES, COSTS, PROFIT, STOCK, LEADS, REPEAT BUYERS)

Month:
Book title or catalog:

1. SALES
   Total units sold (retail):
   Total units sold (wholesale):
   Total units sold (consignment):
   Total revenue:
   Top channel by revenue:
   Top channel by units:
2. COSTS
   Printing/production costs:
   Shipping/logistics costs:
   Design/editing costs (if monthly portion):

Marketing costs:
Event costs:
Total costs:
3. PROFIT
   Gross profit (revenue - direct costs):
   Net profit (revenue - all costs):
   Profit margin percent:
4. STOCK
   Starting stock:
   New stock added:
   Ending stock:
   Dead stock notes (slow locations or items to retrieve):
5. LEADS AND PARTNERSHIPS
   New bulk leads contacted:
   Bulk deals closed:
   New shops added:
   New schools/organizations added:
   Upcoming events scheduled:
6. REPEAT BUYERS AND COMMUNITY
   Repeat buyers this month:
   Email list growth:
   Top reader questions received:
   Top feedback themes:
7. NEXT MONTH ACTIONS (TOP 5)

1.
2.
3.
4.
5.

Final note on using these tools

Do not try to use all tools perfectly on day one. Start with two: the One-Page Plan and the Monthly Scorecard. Those two alone can make you behave like a publisher. As you grow, add the inventory tracker and the metadata worksheet. Then add the scripts and agreements.

A business grows when the tools become habits.

FINAL NOTE TO THE READER

If you reached this point, it means you did more than read. You stayed. And staying matters, because most people start a dream and abandon it halfway. A book business is not built by talent alone. It is built by staying long enough for the work to mature.

I wrote this book because I have lived the gap between "I want to write" and "I want my writing to feed me." That gap is full of confusion, delays, fear, and sometimes poverty. Many good writers remain stuck there for years, not because they are lazy, but because no one taught them the business side in simple language.

I want you to remember one thing above all.

You do not need to be famous to earn from books.
You need to be clear, consistent, and commercially wise.

If you take the lessons in this book seriously, your results may not explode overnight, but they will grow. A calm book business grows like a tree. It does not shout while it grows, but one day people stand under its shade and wonder how it became so strong.

So do not worship launch week. Do not chase applause. Do not compare your beginning to someone else's middle. Build your catalog one brick at a time. Print with discipline. Sell with respect. Train others. Document your system. Keep your integrity clean. And never forget that a book is a tool meant to serve people, not a trophy meant to stroke your ego.

If you ever feel tired, return to the simplest cycle.

Create.
Package.
Distribute.
Sell.
Repeat.

That cycle will carry you when motivation fails.

I am grateful you chose to learn with me. Now go build. Your readers are not a myth. They are real people with real needs. They are waiting for someone to speak clearly and deliver value. Be that person.

LEAVE A REVIEW REQUEST

If this book helped you, I have one favor to ask.

Please leave an honest review where you bought it.

A short review is enough. Even two or three sentences help.

Reviews are not only for my ego. Reviews help other readers decide quickly whether this book is the right fit. They also help the store show the book to people who need it.

If you do not know what to say, you can use one of these simple formats:

Option 1:
What problem were you facing?
What did this book help you do?

Option 2:
What chapter helped you most and why?

Option 3:
Who would you recommend this book to?

Thank you for supporting the work. Your review is part of how this book reaches more people.

BULK ORDERS AND TRAINING USE

If you want to use this book for a school, church, organization, office training, or reading club, you can order in bulk.

Bulk orders are available for:
Student programs and classroom use
Church leadership and discipleship groups
NGO and community training programs
Office teams and staff development
Workshops, seminars, and events
Reader clubs and youth groups

Training use permission:
You are allowed to use short excerpts for teaching and discussion, as long as you do not reproduce large sections or distribute the full content without permission. If you need special permission for photocopies, translation, or program licensing, contact me first so we can agree on clear terms.

For bulk orders, partnerships, or training licensing, reach out using the contact details below:

Email: maluthabiel@gmail.com
Website: www.johnshalom.com
Phone/WhatsApp: +211 927 145 394

ABOUT THE AUTHOR

John Monyjok Maluth (Panyim) is a writer, teacher, and publisher who believes books are not only for inspiration but also for survival, growth, and economic freedom. He writes and teaches with a practical focus, helping ordinary people turn knowledge into outcomes through clear systems, disciplined habits, and ethical business thinking.

His work is shaped by a life that has moved through hardship, displacement, and constant rebuilding. Those experiences taught him that meaning without structure collapses, and structure without meaning becomes empty. So he builds both. He teaches readers to treat books as tools, to treat writing as a craft, and to treat publishing as a serious business that can serve people with dignity.

John's mission is empowerment. His value is integrity. His vision is inspiration.

www.ingramcontent.com/pod-product-compliance
Lightning Source LLC
Chambersburg PA
CBHW031613210526
45464CB00004B/1557